The Purchase
of Paradise

STUDIES IN SOCIAL HISTORY

edited by
HAROLD PERKIN
Professor of Social History, University of Lancaster

For a list of books in the series see back endpaper

THE PURCHASE
OF PARADISE

Gift Giving and the Aristocracy, 1307–1485

Joel T. Rosenthal

Department of History,
State University of New York, Stony Brook, New York

LONDON: Routledge & Kegan Paul
TORONTO: University of Toronto Press

First published 1972 in Great Britain by
Routledge & Kegan Paul Limited
and in Canada and the United States of America by
University of Toronto Press
Toronto and Buffalo
Printed in Great Britain by
C. Tinling & Co. Ltd.
London and Prescot
RKP ISBN 0 7100 7262 7
UTP ISBN 0 8020 1889 0
UTP Microfiche ISBN 0 8020 0229 3

for
Lee,
who correctly thought that
gossip was the best part of
History

Contents

Tables

Preface

THIS work is an introduction to one aspect of the social history of the English nobility in the later middle ages. I have chosen to examine some of the forms of gift giving between the aristocracy and the church in order to see what an analysis of one particular form of social action can tell us about the givers and the recipients. Gift giving has been chosen because, as a form of semi-voluntary activity, it gets us well away from the oft-covered grounds of baronial politics and economics. It also forces us to work with such concepts as the family and regional favouritism, and thus to re-examine their definition and their validity. I believe that only functional or behavioural studies such as this, rather than abstract definitions, can show us more exactly the framework of the ideas and institutions in which men and women worked in the middle ages. I also believe that, in a field of historical inquiry for which data is hardly abundant, group studies such as this, using simple statistics, offer a variety of insights not available in other ways. Historians who begin their books by announcing that a pioneer work is to follow have always puzzled me. I am content to say that since no one else has chosen to do a study like the one that follows, I have had the pleasure of working at it at various times for the past five years.

I owe many debts for this work, though both in conception and in execution I take full responsibility. The Social Science Research Council was generous enough to support me during a leave of absence from my teaching studies. The Research Foundation of the State University of New York and the American Philosophical Association also gave me tangible support, and the Institute of Historical Research was a generous host, not for the first or last time. Professor

Lucy Mair, E. M. Carus-Wilson, F. R. H. DuBoulay, Sylvia Thrupp, and James L. Cate all provided encouragement and support. Professor Herbert S. Klein was a kind and helpful critic. My wife has tried, for several years, to teach me what an historical table is supposed to convey to the reader. I hope her efforts show to some avail: if they do not, I am the opaque window and must take the blame accordingly.

New York   J. T. ROSENTHAL
1971

Abbreviations

CPL	*Calendar of Papal Letters*
CPR	*Calendar of Patent Rolls*
Fifty Earliest English Wills	*Fifty Earliest English Wills:* F. J. Furnivall (ed.), Early English Text Society, old series, 78 (1882)
Gibbons	*Early Lincoln Wills*, A. W. Gibbons (ed.), (Lincoln, 1888)
Jacob	*The Register of Henry Chichele:* E. F. Jacob (ed.), (Oxford, 1938), vol. 2, wills
K & H	D. Knowles and R. N. Hadcock: *Medieval Religious Houses in England and Wales* (London, 1953)
Monasticon	Sir Wm. Dugdale: *Monasticon Anglicanum*, J. Caley, H. Ellis, and B. Bandinel (eds.), (London, 1817–30), Six volumes
North Country Wills	*North Country Wills*, J. W. Clay (ed.), Surtees Society, vol. 116 (1908)
PCC	Wills proved before the Prerogative Court of Canterbury, preserved in the Principal Probate Registry, Somerset House
Repingdon	*Register of Bishop Philip Repingdon, 1405–1419*, M. Archer (ed.), Lincoln Record Society LVII and LVIII
RW	*A Collection of All the Wills . . . of the Kings and Queens of England, etc.*, J. Nichols (ed.), (London, 1780).
Somerset Wills	*Somerset Medieval Wills*, F. W. Weaver (ed.), Somerset Record Society, XVI (1901)

TE	*Testamenta Eboracensia*, J. Raine and J. Raine jr (eds), Surtees Society, vols 4, 30, 45, and 53: volumes of *TE* are numbered I, II, III, and IV
Test. Karl.	*Testamenta Karleolensia*, R. S. Ferguson (ed.), Cumberland and Westmorland Antiquarian and Archaeological Society, extra series, IX (1893)
TRHS	*Transactions of the Royal Historical Society*
TV	*Testamenta Vetusta:* N. H. Nicolas (ed.), (London, 1826), two volumes
VCH	*Victoria County History*
Wills and Inventories	*Wills and Inventories illustrative of the Northern Counties of England*, J. Raine (ed.). Surtees Society, vol. 2 (1835), part 1

1

Introduction

THE fourteenth and fifteenth centuries were a golden age for the English nobility. Their role in government and society was both prominent and respected. They were an integral part of the decision-making process of the king's government. Most developments in the constitutional history of the day either came at their behest or as part of a royal reaction against the interference of these over-mighty subjects. Foreign policy was formulated in large part to suit their interests —to divert them from domestic and dynastic crises, and to give them opportunities to flex their military, economic and chivalric muscles in foreign fields. What freedom of action the king did gain between 1307 and 1485 came as much by playing different factions of the nobility off against each other as it came through the support of such non-noble sources of power as the towns, gentry, professional civil service, and the men who rose via the meritocracy of the church. These assertions about the role of the nobles in government are hardly in dispute, and a respected short history of medieval England treats this period in chapters entitled 'Monarchy versus Aristocracy' and 'The Decline and Fall of Feudalism'.[1]

Aristocratic domination of the countryside was no less marked. 'Local government' is the phrase we apply to the story of how the king's peace and fund-raising machinery worked when set in the

---

[1] H. M. Cam: *England Before Elizabeth* (London, 1950), chapters 11 and 12, covering the years 1297–1509.

A survey of the recent scholarship on the nobility can be found in the bibliographies of M. McKisack: *The Fourteenth Century* (Oxford, 1959), E. F. Jacob: *The Fifteenth Century* (Oxford, 1961), J. R. Lander: *Conflict and Stability in Fifteenth Century England* (London, 1968), and R. L. Storey: *The End of The House of Lancaster* (London, 1967).

particular context of a locality, its inhabitants, and its peculiar institutions and mores. In practice, to study local history and society is often to illuminate the way in which the great magnates in the counties controlled elections to Parliament, selected or dominated the selections of the sheriffs, coroners, escheators, and justices of the peace, and simply over-awed and suppressed the king's justice when its independence and objectivity threatened their parochial interests. The sworn retainer and the armed retinue were not peculiar to the fourteenth and fifteenth centuries, but they were ubiquitous trademarks of those years. There is very little whimsy in a map of England during the Wars of the Roses which depicts the realm as divided between the different aristocratic allegiances as a map of the 1640s can do between Parliament and Charles I.[2] And the divisions on the map of the 1460s and 1470s are not too different, in many respects, from those which could have been drawn for the 1320s, the 1370s, or the first fifteen years of the fifteenth century, though the names and families within the peerage showed considerable variation over the years.

The economic dominance of the nobility was almost on a par with the political. Along with the great churchmen, the nobles were the landholders of those vast blocks of territory which monopolized a good deal of the countryside then and which lend themselves now, because of the concentration of record sources, to scholarly inquiry. The creation and prosperity of the aristocratic estates and honours, as administrative and economic complexes, are subjects which have received much attention in recent years. Along with a knowledge of their incomes and their policies as landlords has come a better grasp of how and why the nobles acted as they did in local affairs and, by extension, in national issues. The complex relations between bastard feudalism and economic decline (and its absence), between laws of the king's government and local estate holding and transmission, between local agrarian practices and the needs of great absentee lords, etc., are coming to be appreciated if not fully understood.

In this study we proceed onwards from an assumption of the basic importance of the nobility in fourteenth and fifteenth century England. There is almost no area we can touch in investigating the social history of England that is not under their considerable influence. But

[2] There are numerous such maps, and they serve a useful purpose, see K. H. Vickers: *England in the Later Middle Ages* (London, 1913) end of volume; Storey: *op. cit.*, p. 128 (for the political divisions in 1453–4); S. B. Chrimes: *Lancastrians, Yorkists, and Henry VII* (London, 1966) end of volume.

historians have not done much to create a social history of that medieval nobility.[3] By now we should attempt to say something about them as a group which will add a further dimension to the picture we already have of their political and economic roles. We must begin to deal with the problem of group identity in their society. Can we learn about the existence, tacit or explicit, of common patterns of action and behaviour within a recognized élite, as well as about the relationship between ascribed social roles and private or voluntary realms of endeavour? While we still know very little about these unofficial aspects of aristocratic lives, we will at least here make an attempt at treating these complex issues.

No comprehensive social history of the nobility can yet be written.[4] We shall concentrate in this study upon some selected topics in their private lives, particularly upon some specific aspects of their philanthropic activity, their voluntary gift giving. The specific types of philanthropic activity we will study have not been chosen completely at random, as we shall explain. Firstly, they were widely practised forms of philanthropic activity, and we thereby embrace most of the nobles within our inquiry. Also, the activities were carried out in response to the accepted values of the day, and social history properly commences with the orthodox and conventional rather than with the anomalous or the unique. We are not yet ready to look for the extraordinary. Furthermore, because money and property are involved in the story of gift giving, not just beliefs, the relationship between private values and those of family, political affiliation, and public expectation come to the fore. We may discover considerable tension or variance between what people were supposed to do and what they did. We are not only looking for the gift giving of individual peers, but we are hoping to determine whether they acted in conformity (if not in cooperation) with others of their family, region of the country, and social class. What does their philanthropy reveal about their own bonds of association and of self-identification? Lastly, are there

[3] J. M. W. Bean: *The Decline of English Feudalism* (Manchester, 1968) begins to push us towards a content analysis of legislation with a view on whether the class interests of the aristocratic land-holders were being furthered by legislation. The most instructive specific study of the nobility continues to be G. A. Holmes: *The Estates of the Higher Nobility in Fourteenth Century England* (Cambridge, 1957).

[4] The two greatest compendia for genealogy and family history, basic building blocks from which all studies of the nobility must be largely constructed, are William Dugdale: *The Baronage of England* (London, 1675-6), two volumes, and G. E. Cokayne: *The Complete Peerage*, ed. by Hon. Vicary Gibbs (London, 1910-59), thirteen volumes.

correlations between private and public activity? Were nobles on the way up unusually expansive toward the church and the poor? Or, conversely, were the more expansive nobles the more likely to go up in political fortune (and is the relationship causal or coincidental)? And if these prove to be essentially unrelated factors, what do we learn about the compartmentalization of medieval society?

Because much of this study sails through waters that are yet uncharted, it seems best to set out, in a careful and explicit fashion, some of our working premises. Several points in particular must be clarified lest confusion and ambiguity arise when the data begin to accumulate.

The first issue is our principle of inclusion. Who qualifies for treatment: who is excluded? Who, for our purposes, can be considered noble? Most treatments of the medieval nobility deal with specific families or regions, so the need for a precise yet general definition of the peerage is usually skirted. But the situation is very different when one begins by embracing, as one's subject, all those people within the group. For the fourteenth and fifteenth centuries the matter of definition is of particular importance because we have to work with record sources—mostly wills and the calendared patent rolls—which make no natural distinction between the 'social class' of their subjects. We are left with the necessity of formulating our own definition, on some principle that was not inherently obvious to those who recorded the documents we shall use.[5]

We have chosen to define our subjects as the parliamentary nobility. By 'parliamentary nobility' we mean those men who, between 1307 and 1485, were summoned to sessions of the king's parliament by means of individual writs.[6] With some qualifications, amplified below, this definition serves our purpose. It gives us the bulk of the greatest, wealthiest, and most influential people in the kingdom to work with (or upon), and yet at the same time it removes from our shoulders the need to decide on individual cases on the basis of merit or interest. We

[5] L. Stone: *The Crisis of the Aristocracy, 1558–1641* (Oxford, 1965) treats the question of a functional and ideological distinction between the aristocracy and other ranks in society. But Professor Stone's sources are largely family documents, from families which are unequivocally noble, and he is not forced to decide exactly who, in a series of record sources, is noble and who is not. We must decide exactly whom to include in this quantitative treatment.

[6] By 1307 the nobility was beginning to be differentiated, at least in law, from the inchoate group of 'barons' of the twelfth and thirteenth centuries. And after 1485 the sources for such a study both change in nature and begin to proliferate. Therefore, the fourteenth and fifteenth centuries offer a good intermediary ground, with a discrete peerage, and yet not one separated by the nature of the sources from other laymen.

can assume that *most* of the social, economic, and political élites in England are included within our scope, and that their membership in the parliamentary nobility indicates that their contemporaries shared our recognition of their high status, whether achieved or merely inherited.

This is not the place to explore the qualifications which admitted one to the ranks of the parliamentary nobility. We can ignore the fairness or the precision of the criteria which singled some men out for the receipt of individual writs of summons. Neither need we here worry about distinguishing between those who made the grade and those who just failed to do so. We can merely take the élite lay group, as defined for constitutional purposes, and use it for a social inquiry. It is possible that we might be handed a group so heterogeneous that no valid internal comparisons can be made. But this possibility seems remote, neither is it borne out by the evidence examined below. Furthermore, the obvious alternative would be to work with a group as delineated by us in accordance with some criteria of social status that we determine. If our definition gave us a group substantially different from the parliamentary nobility we would be preferring our own idea of what constituted a medieval élite group to that accepted by the values of the time. If not every great layman of the realm was a noble, at least almost all the nobles were among the great laymen of the realm.

The constitutional history of the peerage and the House of Lords can be found elsewhere.[7] So can discussions of the differences between the English nobility, without separate legal status or caste legislation, and their continental counterparts.[8] We need not worry about what it connoted, in legal and political terms, to be summoned to parliament.[9]

[7] L. O. Pike: *A Constitutional History of the House of Lords* (London, 1894) for a full discussion of the issues. All the standard legal and constitutional histories have something to say, but fail to add much. K. B. McFarlane: 'The English Nobility in the Later Middle Ages', *Proceedings of the International Congress of Historical Sciences* (Vienna, 1965), pp. 337–44, for his last effort to summarize his views on the formation of the medieval nobility.

[8] L. Genicot: 'La Noblesse au Moyen age dans l'ancienne "Francie", Continuité, rupture ou évolution?' *Comparative Studies in Society and History*, V (1962–3), pp. 52–9. A. Goodwin, (ed.) *The European Nobility in the Eighteenth Century* (London, 1953) is good for comparative purposes. For the origins of the medieval nobility, Marc Bloch: *Feudal Society* (Chicago, 1961–2), chapters 21 and 22.

[9] *The Complete Peerage, op. cit.*, I, xxiii: 'So we come back to the crucial question, what constitutes a Parliament for peerage purposes? and this query nobody answers, for nobody knows.' F. W. Maitland: *The Constitutional History of England* (Cambridge, 1908), p. 79: 'Lawyers and antiquaries have been forced to seek for a strict theory of the baronage and have never been very successful in finding one.'

Once received, by the fourteenth century the right to a continuing series of individual writs of summons was becoming hereditary, just as the writ (when first received) was becoming tantamount to a patent of nobility. But the building of these important legal and constitutional bridges is not our concern. Moreover, we make no attempt to distinguish between the various ranks of the nobility. A duke and a simple baron are both considered on a par. For our purposes both were noble.

The constitutional criteria we have accepted were formulated in terms of individuals. However, the functional unit applied to the social data, both in terms of amassing and assessing it, is the family of the man who received the writ of summons, not just the peer himself. By 'family' we mean the nuclear or only slightly extended family, in so far as the sources are clear as to the nature of the relationship. This is often impossible to ascertain, and members of a more extended kin group are doubtlessly included at times. The wives, male children, unmarried daughters, and brothers of the parliamentary nobleman are lumped with the man himself within the family unit. While these members of a peer's family were not noble in the legal or constitutional sense, we make the crucial assumption that they shared a common behavioural pattern with the peer himself. This point is impossible to prove or to refute at this time, and only more behavioural studies of this sort will answer this large question of whether the constitutional nobility was also a social aristocracy.

As a working hypothesis it seems legitimate to accept the family as the unit of organization. The peer was invariably the political and economic leader of his whole family network. It is reasonable to assume that he set the social tone as well. His younger brothers, sons, and nephews accepted his lead in the realm of private and voluntary activity, as they did in politics. We have no reason to believe that these other members of the family consistently acted in opposition to the lead furnished by the peer. When we use the net of family in tallying acts of gift giving we do not include relatives with different surnames, for example, maternal kin, in-laws, married daughters or married sisters (and their children). The patrilineal, patrinomial family is as far as we go. This is in keeping with what we know of English social structure at other social levels.

Within our definition of nobility there are three categories of exceptions. One covers immediate members of the royal family. Though clearly 'noble', they have been excluded. This excision extends to sons, nephews, and grandsons in male descent from the monarch. Actually between 1307 and 1485 there are not many people in this category. We lose a few interesting nobles, e.g. the earls of Lancaster, John of Gaunt, Humphrey of Gloucester, and Richard of York (a great grandson of Edward III and the father of two kings), as well as a good deal of ecclesiastical benefaction.[10] Close proximity to the throne was, however, apt to affect one's social behaviour. The close royal kin were usually so rich and lived such public lives that their incorporation into this study would bias the entire quantitative picture.

Clerics from noble families are also excluded. Their numbers were considerable: about thirty-five of the bishops alone in this period were of aristocratic birth, and a great many more had careers, usually as secular clergymen, which ended just short of the episcopacy. But such men did not generally give to the church from their family's wealth, though they were often quite generous with the personal wealth they accumulated during their careers in the church. Thus in the particular realms of voluntary activity we are concerned with, the clerics were separate from their families, though this was not the case in their political biographies. Accordingly, we treat no churchmen here. They were not functional members of their patrilineal kin groups, at least not when gift giving is the activity under consideration.

The last group of nobles omitted are those who stand as the sole and unique members of their families ever to receive the individual writs of summons. One peer does not make a noble family, at least not for purposes of social history. Possibly during their brief stay within the parliamentary peerage some of them did act up to the standard of 'typical' nobles. But actually most fell far below the 'average' noble standards of gift giving. This is not surprising; a family which could not maintain its grasp on a peerage was only marginally within the desired social circle of wealth and prominence anyway.[11] We should

[10] S. Armitage-Smith: *John of Gaunt* (New York, 1964 reprint) and K. H. Vickers: *Humphrey, Duke of Gloucester* (London, 1907) for these two important figures. More information can be found about Gaunt's ecclesiastical endowment and charities in the volumes of his registers. For York, J. Rosenthal: 'Richard, Duke of York: A Fifteenth Century Layman and the Church', *Catholic Historical Review*, L (1964), pp. 171–87.

[11] Some of the 'occasional peers' who are omitted here engaged in some charitable activity, but quite a few have left no record of relevant activity. Not many were patrons on a large scale. Thomas de Bradeston built a chantry (*CPR 1343–45*, p. 240), and endowed St Augustine's, Bristol (*CPR 1343–45*, p. 373). John de Clavering alienated property to Ritton church (*CPR 1324–27*, p. 47), and to the hospital of St James and St John within his own lordship of Aynho (*CPR 1317–21*, p. 385). Oliver de Ingham, Lord John de Lancaster, John de Orreby, Miles de

note, however, that this principle of exclusion means the nobility we work with may have been wealthier, more powerful, and with a greater tradition of continuity than the actual peerage at any session of parliament ever was, since the real assemblage did include those marginal figures whom we have eliminated. On the other hand this exclusion of the minor peers may balance our exclusion of the royal nobles, and so we are hopefully left with the typical, broad middle ranges of nobles to work with and on whom we will base our conclusions.

As we have defined the personnel of the inquiry, the nobility was hardly a large élite group. Their numbers fluctuate from sixty or seventy men in the early fourteenth century to a fifteenth-century average of thirty-five to fifty.[12] At any moment we are not dealing with more than several hundred people, most of whom have left no individual records. However, these several hundred people, coming from three to six dozen families, did control a great share of the non-royal secular wealth of the kingdom. They offered social leadership to their inferiors, many of whom also lived on their lands and laboured, directly or indirectly, in their service. They were the great men of the realm, and their activities are worthy of our attention if we care to learn how and why medieval men chose the areas of voluntary social activity as a vehicle for self expression.

We should say something here about precisely which social activities we plan to examine in detail. By studying the phenomenon of gift giving we can see the nobles in an area of activity where they had relative freedom, with some opportunity to give what they pleased to recipients of their choice, in a manner and with controls that suited their individual preferences. But it was freedom within a framework of expectations, prescriptions, and demands. Men of property were expected to give to the church and to the poor, during life and at death, both to justify their inequitable status in the social hierarchy and to buy prayers for their own souls. Within this framework of values considerable scope was left for individual initiative. Were the nobles leaders or followers; as we identify and measure the forms and

[12] McFarlaine: *op. cit.*, pp. 338–9.

Stapleton, etc., were all donors to the church, mostly by means of alienations in mortmain of small bits of real property. Piers de Uvedale founded a chantry chapel at Dinham, and John de Kirketon founded All Saints Hospital, Holbeach. Most of these activities belong to the first half of the fourteenth century. Likewise, so do most of the occasional nobles. By Richard II's time membership in the peerage—and individual summonses to Parliaments—was not granted and withdrawn so quixotically.

amounts of their philanthropy, we are also keeping account of the scope left for individuality at the top of the social pyramid.

Within the world of benefaction, there were a limited number of alternatives in regard to the nature of the recipient, the forms of the gift or bequest, and the sources available to us for study. We have chosen to examine five specific forms of medieval charitable activity (and a sixth in an appendix). All the types of activity selected meet two criteria: they are largely knowable through the use of a particular extant source, and they were engaged in by an appreciable number, if not all the nobles. Not all gifts can be dealt with. We limit ourselves to forms of benefaction that can be identified, isolated, and controlled by a peculiar legal or administrative process that is reflected by a particular source, e.g. the need to obtain a royal licence to alienate land in mortmain, or the need to make a will in order to direct the disposition of one's personal possessions after death. Medieval men practised other forms of philanthropy, but these cannot readily be analysed because they were too diffuse or because they were never reflected in a centralized form of source material. In generalizing about social behaviour it is best to work from a specific and a quantitative base. The varieties of gift giving considered below may be but loosely related to each other. Even so, however, they form a first line of evidence from which we can gauge the general propensity of the lay élite to share its wealth, to control and manipulate society through the use of charity, to channel manpower and money in desired directions, and to accept and to support the orthodox social values. These activities are a guide to what the nobles wished to do, rather than a full treatment of what the church actually did receive, or of how the gift was administered, or of what effect it subsequently had upon the recipient.

We must set out several important considerations about the nature of medieval philanthropy. It is essential that we do not attempt to make any distinction between money and bequests given to the church for what we would today call spiritual purposes, for example the purchase of prayer services, and what we would see as secular charity, for example alms to the poor or to prisoners. Too many scholars have worried over this false distinction.[13] It seeks to separate that which men of the fourteenth and fifteenth centuries bound together as a

---

[13] J. A. F. Thomson: 'Piety and Charity in Late Medieval London', *Journal of Ecclesiastical History*, XVI (1965), p. 180: 'It is often impossible to separate pious gifts from charitable ones, because no such differentiation existed in the mind of the donor.' But the error continues to be made. W. K. Jordan: *Philanthropy in England, 1480–1660* (London, 1959), *passim*.

matter of course. Almost all forms of medieval philanthropy had the purchase of prayers as their ultimate goal, whether they were to be said immediately or in the far-distant future, by laymen, secular priests, canons, monks, friars, or anchorites.[14] Again, almost all forms of medieval gift giving, whatever the ultimate purpose and destination, were administered in the first instance by the church. This is a crucial caveat. The act of giving the gift—be it money, goods, or land —formed the essence of the charitable activity, the social exchange. The act of giving was what impressed the medieval donor. The medieval mind (and social conscience) made no distinction between an eventual sacerdotal and a social end of charity. So to avoid a serious anachronism, we make no differentiation below between ecclesiastical endowments and outright charity. All forms of gift giving were part of a unified spectrum of activity, the economic end of which was usually to transfer goods from lay to ecclesiastical hands.

Gift giving was but part of a larger exchange, that of services and obligations in return for money and goods, which we recognize as the specialization of labour. Philanthropy was but a part of an interconnected system of social relationships and reciprocities. What is said about the symbolic and extended nature of gift giving in traditional societies is relevant here: the moral nature of the economic transaction, the representative role of those affecting the actual transaction, standing as they do for larger groups and networks of individuals, the continuing nature of the tie between giver and recipient, the competition between many systems of loyalty and obligation, etc.[15] The bifurcation of the world into the sacred and the profane is a relevant concept here—it helps to explain in part why the active role in philanthropy remained with the church, and why the lay donors were so passive in terms of exercising social control.

We must keep all these considerations before us, and judge neither medieval charity nor medieval man by modern standards. If we view the nobles as part of a great chain of being, running from their creator-saviour through themselves and down to their descendants and menials, we can better grasp the social and spiritual milieu in which their charity was given and received.

---

[14] An abbot acknowledged that 'the offering of the prayers of the brethren is the sole return we can make for the kindness shown to us': G. Baskerville: *English Monks and the Suppression of the Monasteries* (London, 1937) p. 20.

[15] M. Mauss: *The Gift* (transl., I. Cunnison) (New York, 1967, written 1925). E. E. Evans-Pritchard reminds us that we have lost 'by the substitution of a rational economic system for a system in which exchange of goods was not a mechanical but a moral transaction': p. ix.

2

<hr />

Prayers for the dead

<hr />

W E have said that medieval philanthropy was not a simple matter of impersonal benefaction. The giving of the gift activated a complicated mechanism of social exchange, with the church diverting its personnel and shaping its structures, duties, and teachings so as to offer the laymen a fair reciprocity for their money, obedience, and acceptance of the prescribed ecclesiastical values. In this chapter we shall examine the conditions laymen attached to the direct purchase of prayers, with an eye on both what we can learn about their relations with the church and about social structure and the values of the laity.

There are two bodies of Christian doctrine which are relevant to our concerns here. One covers the church's teachings about charity, poverty, and the need to share one's worldly riches. The other doctrine relates to the teachings about purgatory and the redemptive value of prayers for the souls of the dead.[1] The concept of purgatory gained in the popular religious imagination in the later middle ages. More and more of the church's efforts were devoted to teaching the living what they could do for the dead—both the donor himself, and any other he sought to aid. Popular religion largely focused on this one chapter in the entire corpus of Christian belief. As well as occupying the time and efforts of the clergy, the concern with purgatory consumed a con-

---

[1] Discussions of the doctrine of purgatory concentrate upon whether the doctrine stems directly from patristic times or whether it is a product of eleventh and twelfth century thought, and they emphasize the distinction between the official teachings and popular thought. As the teachings came across to the laity, believers thought they could lighten the sufferings of purgatory by four means: masses, prayers of the saints (the treasury of merit), alms, and fasts. Hastings: *Encyclopaedia of Religion and Ethics* (New York, 1955), I, 212, and *Dictionnaire de Théologie Catholique* (Paris, 1936), XIII, part 1, column 1163–1357.

siderable part of the laity's money and spiritual enthusiasm. Whatever individual religious beliefs and convictions were found among the English peerage, there certainly was no lack of support for the institutionalized aspects of endowment and prayer that could enhance one's chances of eternal salvation.

In this chapter we shall analyse the conditions and terms governing endowments of prayers that were enunciated by the nobles when they procured royal licences to alienate property into mortmain, and when they wrote their wills. Apart from the interest these instructions carry for students of liturgy, the regulation of prayer services has been much neglected. It is an extremely fertile source for social history, containing much information about family networks and relationships, as well as material revealing the extent of lay knowledge of and concern with the religious services so familiar to medieval man. This investigation rests upon the premise that when one pays to support and to perpetuate the institutions of the day, one is actively embracing them. The degree and amount of involvement may vary greatly with different individuals, ranging from mere passive acceptance of conventional *mores* to a deep, conscious, and explicit commitment. But regardless of where on the spectrum a given figure stood, when he paid his money and gave his instructions governing the recitation of prayers, he was both supporting the accepted system and striving to carve his niche within it.

This aspect of the realm of endowed and directed prayers is particularly seen to be part of the social system of (balanced) reciprocities between laymen and clerics, a chapter in the division of labour in a society where all accepted the rightness of an order in which some fought, some worked, and some prayed. All organized religions accept some degree of specialization of labour. Medieval Christianity, however, was singularly committed to such a scheme. It had both a celibate priesthood, excluded from 'normal' life in the world, and a laity which was doctrinally prohibited from performing the sacraments necessary for salvation. Each had a basic need of the other, for in this biological-spiritual 'ecosystem' neither group was self-sustaining. This rigid specialization of labour was made all the more obvious by the hierarchical and segmentary social structure of the day.

Seen in this way, it is no wonder that the laity supported with such zeal the role accorded them in the cosmic order. They subsidized a vast complex of clerks, all of whom were willing to take their money and in return offer prayers for their souls. Both lay and clerical actions are readily understood when we remember the limited amount of control and initiative accorded the layman[2] in the quest for salvation:

> The popular view of the mass was distinctly mechanical . . . The Layman was taught to believe that he could increase the effect of Eucharistic prayers by the simple process of multiplying them and making them more elaborate. The benefits which the living and dead received varied in direct proportion with the number of masses said and the amount of offering made at each.

While prayers could be said for the good estate of the living, they were most grandly subsidized when directed toward the redemption of the dead. If adequately endowed, prayers for the dead could be said in perpetuity. They could be celebrated simultaneously in many institutions and by numerous priests within each institution.

They could be said for whomsoever the patron chose. Through them one could and did aid the spiritual welfare of relatives, friends, allies, benefactors, beneficiaries, and perhaps all other Christian souls, known and unknown. They could be tailored to express the personal wishes of the patron. It was the donor who[3] 'decided which of his relations and friends should be prayed for, and by what prayers: and he could even prescribe the precise words in which his priest should bid those hearing the mass to add their prayers for the founder's soul'. But beneath this predilection for individuality there was a tendency to follow the fashionable and the orthodox. Endowed prayers were usually meant to be said frequently, 'divine service daily' being the formula found on most of the mortmain licences which carried such directions. The prayers were most commonly said by chantry chaplains or by clerics attached to corporate bodies, rather than by parish priests. The endowments of the laity were a major source of income and a form of visibly useful employment for the clergy. As such they constituted one of the financial premises underlying and buttressing the whole system of corporate ecclesiastical institutions. Did the church have so many priests to satisfy the demands of an aggressive laity, or were the laity encouraged to subsidize prayers in order to support the multitude of priests? The profitability of the doctrine of purgatory to the church certainly did not militate against its promulgation. Reformers were always ready to say that the individually subsidized prayers drew trained and

---

[2] B. L. Manning: *The People's Faith in the Time of Wyclif* (Cambridge, 1919), p. 73.

[3] K. L. Wood-Legh: 'Some Aspects of the History of Chantries in the later Middle Ages', *TRHS*, 4th series, XXVIII (1946), p. 49.

needed men away from their proper parochial responsibilities, and they emphasized a concern for self over social utility. Whatever the truth of this charge, most laymen had little trouble fitting into the orthodox system, both with their convictions and their money.

In the fourteenth and fifteenth centuries the king's government granted the nobles 446 licences to alienate in mortmain, enabling them to grant property to some branch of the church. Of this total, some 360 licences contained specific provisions for the alienation of property to a specific recipient. On 34 per cent of this latter total the noble seeking the licence actually stipulated that he wanted prayers said in return for his gift, and on most of these 121 licences he went so far as to name the intended beneficiaries of the prayers.

By virtue of the patron's right to name the people mentioned in the prayers, his money was being directly translated into other worldly power, through a clerical intermediary. When the payment was made the patron was free to include as many of his fellows as he chose. He could court favour among the living by openly announcing that his concern for their welfare would end neither with his death nor with theirs. He could elaborate lists of relatives and friends, living and dead, and even conclude by mentioning that the souls of all faithful departed would be included. But in contrast to this magnanimous orientation, many nobles had a different interpretation of the prayers, which after all can be viewed as the most precious and lasting tribute one Christian could pay another. The dilution of their efficacy was to be avoided. Too many names, too thinly-spread services, too little endowment—all might serve to make them less potent. Furthermore, inclusion of names of the living might seem safe enough now, but it could prove to be indiscreet following a political *volte face* or a family feud. So whatever the reasons, many nobles implicitly held the view that the fewer people one named, the greater the impact of the prayers (and the safer the political repercussions). Emphasis and comprehensiveness were mutually contradictory. If a choice had to be made, most nobles chose to err in favour of the former, and to limit the list of beneficiaries.

The narrowest, indeed the most selfish stipulation of prayers was that exclusively concerned with the donor; for his good estate while alive, and then only for his own soul. In the licences to alienate this was not a common form of prescribed exchange, though it is found occasionally in the wills. Even the flexible standards of decent Christian charity make this egocentric practice look a bit too exclusive. John Willoughby was the sole beneficiary of the prayer services he endowed within the chapel of Saltfleet Haven, Lincoln,[4] and both Gilbert Umfraville and Thomas Berkeley made such unsociable provisions.[5] There are also a few instances of a single stipulated beneficiary where it was someone other than the donor himself. Though still a bit narrow, selfishness for the sake of another is a little more acceptable. Henry Percy petitioned for exemptions 'from tallages, aids, watches, and all contributions from tenths and other quota of spiritualities when granted by the commonalty of the kingdom, and tenths or other contributions imposed by the Pope' upon the chapel of St Mary, Semer, if the chaplains of that old Percy family foundation would pray for his mother.[6] He made an endowment to the convent at Sawley 'for chantries and other pious works' for his father's soul.[7] Joan Holland maintained three priests whose only duty was to celebrate for the soul of her late husband, the Earl of Kent.[8] Michael de la Pole supported a chaplain in Wingfield parish church, to the extent of £8 per annum, exclusively for the soul of his brother Richard.[9]

But these single-beneficiary licences were unusual: only seven of the 121 licences which specified prayers were so directed (Table 1). Most licences named the donor and at least one other person. Two licences out of every three (80 of 121) named a member of the benefactor's immediate family, and many named more than one person. Wives and parents (usually specified separately as mother and father rather than combined as parents[10]) were the relatives most commonly mentioned. And since many licences were actually issued to the husband and wife jointly, more noblewomen were beneficiaries of prayers than the table indicates, for the rubric 'wife' only indicates that she was a beneficiary when she appears separately and is explicitly mentioned rather than when she was a co-recipient of the licence. When parents are named, they are almost always the *husband's* parents. There are only a few exceptions to this, where a married couple

[4] *CPR 1334–38*, p. 551.
[5] *CPR 1340–43*, p. 432; *CPR 1348–50*, p. 49.
[6] *CPR 1327–30*, p. 482.
[7] *CPR 1354–58*, p. 349.
[8] *CPR 1401–05*, p. 31.
[9] *CPR 1404–08*, p. 141.
[10] Perhaps the term 'parents' was infrequently used because of the wide instance of remarriage and the small likelihood that both parents would be alive. An investigation of kinship terminology as used in the wills and in papal dispensations would be instructive.

TABLE 1   Beneficiaries of prayers named on licences to alienate

Beneficiaries	Fourteenth century	Fifteenth century	Total
Wife	13	8	21
Husband	4	5	9
Mother and father	5	10	15
Mother	7	0	7
Father	5	1	6
Step-parents	1	1	2
Wife and one parent	4	1	5
Children	3	2	5
Siblings	2	2	4
Other kinsmen	5	0	5
(Sub-total)	49	30	79
Ancestors	55	11	66
Descendants	27	3	30
King and royal family	18	27	45
Other named people	8	9	17
Friends and benefactors	2	5	7
All Christians	11	3	14
Total	170	88	258
(Total number of licences)	79	42	121

clearly named the *wife's* parents on the licence, and there are a few
ambiguous cases. A wife's parents presumably had to be taken care
of by her brothers, at least so far as the licences to alienate indicate.
'Husband' in the table refers to the dead husband of the widow
receiving the licence. Women, even noble women, rarely acted as
individual petitioners for a licence while they had a living husband.
The husband acted for the couple. Even when she remarried, the
licence might be given to the woman and her new husband so that
they could jointly alienate the dower she held from the first husband,
so that his soul was provided for with his widow's share of his own
wealth, which was justice of a sort. In all, sixty-four licences (53 per
cent of all the relevant ones) named the spouse and/or the parents
among the beneficiaries. There are two licences which were generous
enough to include step-parents. This is in marked contrast to a pattern

of behaviour which named siblings, alive or dead, on only four licences.

The conclusion to be drawn from Table 1 is that family feelings were strongly vertical, i.e. directly up and down the lineage from generation to generation. They were rarely focused in a horizontal fashion, i.e. on the relatives within the grantor's own generation. Nieces, nephews, uncles, aunts, and cousins (and in-laws)—the horizontal and slightly extended family—are almost never referred to. Their own children were doubtlessly expected to pray for them, rather than the children of their brothers and sisters. If this finding is generally applicable, we can sympathize with the plight of the childless, the unmarried, and the sole survivor. Only five licences bought prayers for all the relatives and kinsfolk; a far smaller number than those which merely named all Christian souls. Collateral lines of the family might be political allies, but they could not be counted on when thoughts turned to the serious business of eternity. Spiritually, if not politically, the family was a nucleated one. Primogeniture and the restriction of peerage to the eldest direct male heir both contributed to this narrowing. These findings run counter to views which emphasize the political role of the large family-oriented blocks of intermarried aristocrats, for example the Lancastrian alliance in Edward II's day, or the Yorkist affiliation of the 1450s and 1460s. In some important respects these larger blocks counted for little, and the real ties of affection and sympathy were confined to much closer relationships.[11]

When a nobleman's son moved into the parliamentary peerage through marriage to an heiress of a great house (who would be considered as a peerless *suo jure* by modern reckoning) he was apt to shift his allegiance from his old kin group to his new. Younger sons might leave the paternal family if an advantageous marriage tied them to their in-laws. In this context the husband of an heiress could cut himself off from his brothers, paternal uncles, etc., and this transfer of allegiance can be indicated by the purchase of prayers. Can we then say that the patterns of prayer endowments reveal a narrowness in the family which would have worked to weaken its effectiveness?

[11] H. R. Trevor-Roper: *Men and Events* (New York, 1957), pp. 31–2: 'Why must the tomb be prefabricated, the masses prepaid? It is because, in spite of all this lip-service to the family, no one really trusted anyone else, not even his sons, once his power over them was gone. In reality, the family was not cultivated as such: it was a necessary alliance from which every man hoped individually to profit . . . Such an alliance was cultivated only so long as it served its purpose.'

This perhaps seems a little extreme. On the other hand an extended family within the peerage was apt to be so vast that it embraced people on all sides of any controversy, and so while it might be politically useful it was also so amorphous as to be without any unifying principle of affection. Perhaps the limits of the web of kinship seen here merely indicate a recognized distinction between public business, embracing the extended family, and private business, largely confined to the nuclear family and functionally defined along lines of vertical descent.

A general reference to one's ancestors and progenitors appears on 55 per cent of all the licences (66 of 121). This concern for the salvation of those who have gone before is in striking contrast to the indifference shown towards so many of one's contemporaries even within one's family. However, relatives beyond the immediately preceding generation were rarely mentioned by name or by specific relationship. Strong as the bonds of feeling were—and the fact that the prayers were being paid for is some indication of this—almost no one explicitly named his grandparents. On the other hand, concern for those already dead was much greater than that for those yet to come. Only 25 per cent of the licences (30 of 121) mention heirs and successors. Just five licences talk of children, and these were mostly children who had predeceased their parents, rather than prayers projected into an indefinite future.

Many licences mention the royal family. Of course, a petition to chancery asking to be allowed to make an alienation was not less likely to be granted if the king's good estate and immortal soul were mentioned. Nevertheless, both the number of licences with such a mention and the variety of detail are worthy of our attention. Of all licences issued, 37 per cent mention the royal family; after 1399 64 per cent of those issued did so. No one else—neither parents, ancestors, heirs, dead husbands nor wives, friends nor benefactors—was mentioned nearly this often. Many of the fifteenth-century licences were granted for purposes of subsidizing a new foundation and original endowment. Frequently these licences only carry the monarch's name and that of the grantor(s). But even in the fourteenth century the king, alone or with others of his family, was specified more often than any other single person or relative. When so many were willing to endow prayers for him as an ordinary ingredient of popular religion, it is no wonder that the more beloved medieval rulers were often advanced for canonization.

The first licence issued to a nobleman with the provision for prayers for the king came at the very beginning of Edward II's reign, for his late father.[12] Common formulae on the licences ran 'for the souls of the king's progenitors, kings of England', 'the souls of the king's progenitors, sometime kings of England', 'for the good estate of the king (and) . . . for the soul of the king when he shall have departed this life, and the souls of his progenitors and heirs', etc.[13] A licence granted to Roger Mortimer in 1328 called for divine service to be said for the souls of the king and queens Isabella and Philippa; mention of Edward II is conspicuous by its absence.[14] On the other hand, the licence granted to Thomas Berkeley in Edward III's time explicitly dealt with the king's predecessors and successors.[15] Berkeley did not appreciate his notoriety for his role in Edward II's death, and this alienation was an investment in both public relations and spiritual succour. He was licensed to alienate a messuage, 4 acres of land, 10 of meadow, and 40s annual rent to buy the prayers.

In the fifteenth century the royal family was brought into two of every three licences which called for prayers. The dynastic uneasiness which hung over the realm after 1399 may have heightened any sense of impermanence the nobles occasionally felt about the social order, and prayers for the king may have been a form of self-reassurance. Whatever the cause, through their endowed prayers the nobles sought to ingratiate themselves with an insecure monarchy. They not only included the king in their endowed prayers, but they showed more precision in naming members of his family than they did with their own. Henry V was popular, and two licences issued shortly after his death mentioned him along with his successor.[16] A licence of 1437 spoke of 'Henry V and all his progenitors', to the exclusion of Richard II.[17] All three Lancastrian kings were mentioned by name on a licence granted to the countess of Westmorland.[18] A mention of the king and queen and the king's progenitors reminds us sharply of how the queen was only peripherally within the royal lineage.[19] In the 1450s the Earl

---

[12] *CPR 1307–13*, p. 400.
[13] *CPR 1317–31*, p. 559; *CPR 1330–34*, pp. 39, 265; *CPR 1334–38*, p. 501; *CPR 1361–64*, p. 265.
[14] *CPR 1327–30*, p. 343; *CPR 1381–85*, pp. 411–12.
[15] *CPR 1334–38*, p. 395.
[16] *CPR 1422–29*, pp. 189–90, 347.
[17] *CPR 1436–41*, pp. 55–6.
[18] *CPR 1436–41*, p. 137.
[19] *CPR 1446–52*, p. 82.

of Arundel, as a co-founder of the gild of St Mary at Horsham, endowed prayers for the king, queen, and Prince Edward.[20] A Yorkist partisan such as Lord Hastings ordered prayers for Edward IV, his consort Elizabeth, Queen of England, and their descendants.[21] The Duke and Duchess of Suffolk, in a conciliatory vein, helped support a chaplain to pray for the king, queen, and Edward of Wales.[22]

Of thirteen licences issued under the Yorkist kings which named specific individuals other than the donor, the king appears on ten. The new dynasty was as insecure as the Lancastrian, and it was even more suspicious, and justifiably so, of many noble families. This fashion of the day sounds to us like one born of troublous times. The practice was too prevalent for it to be a simple or reliable gauge of political loyalty; usage had worn out any deep meaning for those who followed the custom. Praying for the king was always a good idea, and many who would subsidize prayers for him were less than eager to fight for him.

People beside the king were mentioned. The souls of all faithful departed, or of all Christians, were sometimes included. This general sweep often went with a specific phrase about heirs and ancestors.[23] All friends and benefactors sometimes came in for mention. On a few licences non-relatives are specified. Some people so honoured were of little significance, being friends or co-benefactors of local ecclesiastical foundations. But the great and the powerful were also included upon occasion: John of Gaunt, Henry Beaufort ('cardinal of England'),[24] master James Goldwell, protonotary apostolic and dean of the cathedral church of Salisbury,[25] Richard Duke of York, William Lord Lovel, and others.[26] The inclusion of these great names, like that of the king, struck donors as a safe practice. The names found are of people considered important by the man paying for the prayers, and he would have been most unusual had he engaged in this spiritual activity without regard to his role in this world. Patterns of family affection, self-consciousness, and old debts must be weighed against more mundane considerations.

Another way of evaluating this quantitative material is by analysing

[20] *CPR 1452–61*, p. 414.
[21] *CPR 1467–77*, p. 372.
[22] *Ibid.*, p. 417.
[23] *CPR 1343–45*, p. 56.
[24] *CPR 1436–41*, p. 137.
[25] *CPR 1467–77*, p. 306.
[26] *CPR 1477–85*, p. 386.

the frequency, in percentages, with which different beneficiaries of the endowed prayers were named on the licences (Table 2). In the fourteenth century, of all the 170 beneficiaries named, specific near relatives made up 29 per cent of the total, ancestors in general 32 per cent, descendants 16 per cent, the king and the royal family 11 per cent, all others 11 per cent. The great shift in the fifteenth century was away from the category of ancestors, and toward the royal family. The former category fell to 12 per cent, the latter rose to 31 per cent (each showing the same change, that of 20 per cent, though in opposite directions). The naming of one's descendants also trailed off sharply, from 16 per cent of the beneficiaries to an insignificant 3 per cent. But other individuals, usually political allies and economic partners, were now mentioned 10 per cent of the time, rather than 5 per cent.

The proportion of near kin to all others named remained almost identical, being 29 per cent in the fourteenth century, 33 per cent in the fifteenth. For the basically nuclear family there was no appreciable change in this regard, but other pulls on the benefactors fluctuated with changing political pressures and *mores*. We must remember that in the fifteenth century the aristocracy were more concentrated around the throne, and so the king was understandably named more often. But we are also dealing with a smaller, more ingrown peerage. These men would have more opportunity to know the king, and each other, and so the higher proportion of their names is explicable in this way. Perhaps this represented a shift toward immediate priorities, away from an equal regard for ancestors and descendants. These latter groups could be placated in other ways, e.g. in one's will, while potential political allies could not be kept waiting in the same fashion. Even the realities of familial obligation might be tied to immediate political and financial need.

We can also contrast the behaviour indicated in the licences to alienate with that shown in the wills, made when nobles were on or near their deathbeds. Unlike the licences from chancery, the wills cannot readily be tabulated. We have no idea what proportion have survived. Furthermore, wills lack the uniformity of form and style which mark an official government document.[27] All licences to alienate generally tell us much the same thing, while some wills are so brief they only commend their maker's soul to God, and yet others fill pages with their elaborate provisions. But despite these limitations, it is

---

[27] Michael M. Sheehan: *The Will in Medieval England*, Pontifical Institute of Medieval Studies, no. 6 (Toronto, 1963).

TABLE 2 Percentage of beneficiaries of prayers named on licences to alienate

Beneficiary*	% in fourteenth century	% in fifteenth century	% Total
Wife	8	9	8
Husband	2	6	3
Mother and father	3	11	6
Mother	4	0	3
Father	3	1	2
Step-parents	1	1	1
Wife and one parent	2	1	2
Children	2	2	2
Siblings	1	2	2
Other kinsmen	3	0	2
(Sub-total)	29	33	31
Ancestors	32	12	26
Descendants	16	3	12
King and royal family	11	31	17
Other named people	5	10	6
Friends and benefactors	1	6	3
All Christians	6	3	5
Total %	100	98†	100

* The nature of the relationship is sometimes ambiguous and medieval kinship terminology is often unclear.

† This column does not equal 100 per cent because of rounding error.

possible to make some contrasts in the behaviour as revealed in the licences and in the wills. This contrast is between behaviour of men (and, to a lesser extent, women) in the full course of their worldly activities and people at or near the moment of death. The spiritual values expressed by those with a place to make in the world are surely qualified and conditioned by their double interest.[28]

The situation was different when one came to make one's will. 'In the late Middle Ages it was customary to say that the man who had made a will had not long to live.'[29] In Nicolas's *Testamenta Vetusta*

[28] *Ibid.*, p. 232.
[29] *Ibid.*, p. 195.

there are about 141 wills of noblemen and members of their families, containing substantial bequests and dating from about 1350 to the end of Richard III's reign. For about 120 of these we have either the date of probate or the date of death. Taking each calendar year as an integer, the interval between the writing of the will and either death or probate averaged 1·13 years. And if two wills with anomalous intervals of eleven and sixteen years are omitted, the interval comes down to 0·92 years. So when the will was written, future opportunities for worldly advancement were apt to be severely limited.[30]

The prevailing patterns for directing prayer services revealed in the licences to alienate also come out in the wills. Perhaps a few more mentioned only themselves in wills: both men and women were culpable on this charge.[31] But the circumstances were different, and perhaps it is well for us to be more charitable, remembering that 'the testator's first thought is not of the transmission of an *hereditas*, but of the future welfare of his immortal soul and his mortal body'.[32] Most wills with stipulations for prayers do mention the testator, his spouse, and his father and mother. As befitted a last will, more dead relatives are now specifically named. By the time of death one might well have outlived several marriage partners. Since the surviving spouse was often an executor, endowments for prayers for previous husbands and wives needed his or her co-operation. Jealousy of former mates was not often a strong force among a class accustomed to arranged and frequent marriages. John Holland named his first wife, Anne, and his surviving one, another Anne, as equal beneficiaries of prayers.[33] Elizabeth Neville, widow of Lord Bergavenny, probably had a record claim: she had buried four husbands, and now requested that a priest pray for the entire group.[34]

Parents were mentioned in the wills as often as on the licences to alienate. Brothers, brothers-in-law, and sisters were now included more frequently. On the deathbed one knew which siblings were already in purgatory, in need of help, and which ones could fend for

---

[30] The short duration between the making of the last will and date of death is confirmed elsewhere. For a group of 30 people, chosen because of the accessibility of the data, the interval was about fifteen months: *Jacob*, p. xl. In a study of the wills of vicars choral, it has been noted 'that very few testators lived more than a week or ten days after they had made their wills'. F. Harrison: *Life in a Medieval College* (London, 1952), p. 398, n. 2.

[31] *TV*, pp. 124, 235, 301.

[32] Pollock and Maitland: *op. cit.*, II, 338.

[33] *TV*, p. 255.

[34] *TV*, p. 441.

themselves; to neglect the former group was unnecessarily churlish. Also, siblings and near in-laws were frequently among one's executors, and their systematic exclusion would have been both offensive and a bad business proposition. Executors could be prodded with intangible as well as with tangible rewards.

Ancestors, predecessors, and progenitors were also mentioned in the wills. The souls of all departed Christians came in for attention more frequently than in the licences. Final thoughts of the immensity of death turned the nobles to consider the company they were soon to join. Heirs and successors were kept in mind a bit less often in the wills than in the licences. The dying may have felt the living could worry about their own salvation. They were concerned more for the well-being of those already dead than for those who were about to outlive them. The living got their compensation in the form of a longer life, and they could partially expiate the inequities of providence by accepting the charge to pray for the testator.

Peeresses made wills, disposing of their often considerable accumulations of possessions and directing their own benefactions and endowments.[35] Whereas the licences to alienate usually mentioned the husband's parents as beneficiaries of the prayers, now the women came into their own. They bought and provided for prayers for their own parents and kin, the previously excluded or ignored in-laws of their husband. When Lady Latimer left £10 for a daily service for 'the remission of the offences of my said Lord and father, and of my Lady my mother', she meant her own father, Richard Beauchamp, and his countess.[36] So again Beatrice Roos's ancestors were not those of her late husband, but rather of her own family.[37] Lady Stafford had the same relations in mind when she made her last testament.[38] The countess of Arundel spoke of 'our parents and ancestors' in this vein,[39] as did other widows. Wills represent a levelling device between the sexes. Women, both widows and those with living husbands, had this last opportunity to redress any neglect which their own family had suffered. It was a last chance to make amends for not having been born male. Restraint and freedom, in their proper places, were both part of a balanced, if unequal, system.

[35] Sheehan: *op. cit.*, pp. 234–41; D. M. Stenton: *The English Woman in History* (London, 1947), pp. 32–4.
[36] *TV*, p. 359.
[37] *TE*, I, 376.
[38] *TV*, p. 166.
[39] *TV*, p. 277.

In contrast to the licences to alienate, the wills almost never mentioned the king or the royal family. There was little change in this between the early fourteenth and the late fifteenth century, whereas there was with the licences. Jasper Tudor, not surprisingly, did bequeath lands to buy prayers for his late wife, Katherine, once married to Henry V, for the Earl of Richmond, and for the 'souls of others my predecessors'.[40] The Countess of Kent still remembered, in 1423, that she wanted prayers said for the souls of Henry IV and Henry V.[41] A famous and rather bold instance of a specific provision was made by Humphrey Bohun, Earl of Hereford. He bought prayers for himself, but to be said at the tomb of Thomas, Earl of Lancaster, at Pontefract. Humphrey's father had fallen while fighting with the Earl.[42] A strongly personalized endowment was that of William, Lord Say, made in 1404:[43] 'Whereas I have been a soldier, and taken wages from King Richard, and the Realm, as well by land as by water, and peradventure, received more than my desert, I will that my executors pay six score marks to the most needful men unto whom King Richard was debtor, in discharge of his soul.' He also endowed prayers for the earls of Arundel and Northumberland, old companions-in-arms. One has a picture of the bluff old soldier, unwilling to neglect a debt of honour, despite a mere dynastic revolution.

Most nobles kept away from the royal family or dangerous friends, and stayed closer to home in their wills. As well as a large sprinkling of in-laws, siblings, and former husbands and wives, they were generous in their mention of friends, benefactors, patrons, and 'good doers'.[44] Richard Poynings was unusual in specifying his grandparents, rather than in merely saying all his ancestors, as most did. He ordered 'masses and trentals for the souls of Sir Michael de Poynings, my honourable Lord and father, my mother, my uncle Richard de Poynings, my grandfather, brothers and sisters, and all my relations, and also for the souls of benefactors, for my own soul, and for all Christian souls'.[45] Anthony Woodville acted in an even more singular fashion when he not only endowed prayers for his wife, Lady Scales, and her brother, but included 'the souls of all the Scales blood'.[46]

[40] *TV*, p. 431.
[41] *TV*, p. 205.
[42] *TV*, p. 68.
[43] *TV*, p. 163.
[44] *TV*, p. 181.
[45] *TV*, p. 123.
[46] *TV*, p. 380.

Household servants were remembered: prayers for the 'souls of all loyal servants' were not uncommon.[47] Thomas Stanley's will enjoined prayers for all 'who died in his or his father's service, or that should die in his service'.[48] Elizabeth Burgh endowed masses for the three husbands she had outlived, plus 'the souls of all my good and loyal servants who have died or may die in my service'.[49] Others speak of more tentative obligations 'to pray for my soul and for the souls of such others as were named upon agreement made betwixt them',[50] or again prayers were to be said 'for the souls of those for whom I am bound'.[51] Such decisions could be left unmade, with the reminder that money was ultimately to be used 'as it may do the most for the souls'.[52] Sometimes the 'souls of all my friends and good doers' were not to be forgotten.[53]

If the royal family were not frequently mentioned in the wills, allies and associates among the nobles were included, particularly after 1450. Walter Blount requested in 1474 that prayers be said for the Duke of Buckingham, Earl Rivers, and Sir John Woodville.[54] In 1475 John Beauchamp referred to prayers for Sir John Fastolf and Lord Botreaux.[55] The factionalism of these years carried over into the sphere of other-worldly relations and alliances. Family considerations, however, worked against purely political ones, and the former were probably the main theme around which the endowments of prayer were organized.

If we summarize the differences in patterns of prayer endowments in the licences to alienate and in the wills, we see that the wills show more concern for the dead, and more flexibility in including those beyond the vertical and nuclear family. They pay less attention to the royal family and to political expediency and the obvious currying of favour. The deathbed, of course, was both a social leveller and a sobering factor. One's thoughts might easily turn, in times of civil and baronial warfare, to prayers 'for all there soules slayn in the felde'.[56]

[47] RW, p. 29.
[48] Dugdale: Baronage, II, 249.
[49] TV, p. 57.
[50] TV, p. 183.
[51] TV, p. 89. Sheehan: op. cit., p. 59, 'Where provision of prayers and masses was mentioned, it was often left to the executors to make arrangements with those who were to say them.'
[52] North Country Wills, p. 55.
[53] TV, p. 182.
[54] TV, pp. 334–5.
[55] TV, p. 338.
[56] TV, p. 182.

If one did miss the kudos that accrued to the living benefactor when making a deathbed bequest, the sense of responsibility to the living was apt to yield to a sense of power and isolation. As one approached one's end, one moved beyond the possibility of contradiction (except on the part of unco-operative executors). The spiritual side of the relationship between the nobles and the church, usually subordinated within a complex of religio-political interactions, now came to the fore.

This is even more the case when we turn our attention to the actual prayers the nobles ordered to be said. The wills are the major source for this type of information. Only a few licences expressly spoke of the services, though they too could become detailed enough upon occasion:[57] 'Divine service in a chapel . . . to wit, every day a mass of Our Lady with canting, a mass of the Trinity, and a mass of the day or a Requiem with Placebo, Dirige, and commendation and other divine services.' A few licences give direction for annual obits or anniversary services.[58] The wills show us that there was considerable interest in the prayers being bought, and only the tersest ones offered no directions to guide the executors. The specifications ran the gamut from simple references to an obit, anniversary, or daily service, to instructions governing the activities of the hired clerks through the seasons of the year, the hours of the day, the festivals of the calendar, etc. The directions varied widely in their details, and the diversity indicates the wide range of lay opinion regarding the significance and efficacy of favourite prayers.[59] The Earl of Warwick considered the different days of the week the crucial point, and he spelled out different prayers for each day.[60] The Earl of Salisbury left instructions which display a close knowledge of the liturgy.[61]

[57] *CPR 1436–41*, pp. 55–6.
[58] *CPR 1422–29*, p. 347; *CPR 1381–85*, pp. 411–12; *CPR 1330–34*, p. 103; *CPR 1317–21*, p. 39.
[59] Manning: *op. cit.*, pp. 174–5.
[60] *TV*, pp. 231–2: 'Three masses to be sung every day, so long as the world shall endure; one of *Our Lady* with note, according to the Ordinale Sarum; the second without notes of requiem, viz., the Sunday of Trinity, the Monday of the Angels, the Tuesday of St Thomas of Canterbury, the Wednesday of the Holy Ghost, the Thursday of Corpus Christi, the Friday of the Holy Cross, and the Saturday of the Annunciation of Our Lord, for the performance of which I devise XL pounds of land per annum.'
[61] *TV*, pp. 215–16: 'One mass to be celebrated every day for my soul, in a particular place appointed for that purpose, with this collect, "Deus cui proprium, etc"; and I desire that two canons of that house, immediately after the mass of the blessed Virgin be ended before my tomb, shall for ever say the psalm of De

Seasonal changes in prayers were countenanced by the Earl of Arundel: 'I will that they (6 priests and 3 choristers) rise every day in summer at sun-rising, and in winter at break of the day.'[62] Benefactors were aware of how life was conducted within regular houses—they were often dispensed to enter them, and they entered them on royal commissions. So they were familiar with the behaviour and responsibility of the recipients of their directions, and they had a basis on which to assess how faithfully their stipulations would be honoured after death. In a world where the addition in a minister's account was frequently inaccurate, it is of interest to note that the Earl of Warwick called for sixty-seven masses on each of fifteen festivals and then, because this totalled more than 1,000 masses by five, he added that 'Five in the whole (be) excepted.'[63] The Duchess of Gloucester's bequest indicates a vivid visual imagination:[64] 'At each of the said masses, before the priest commences "et ne nos," he pronounces with a loud voice, turning towards the people, "for the soul of Thomas, some time Duke of Gloucester, and Alianore, his wife, and all Christian souls, for charity paternoster".' We can picture the duchess, for years before her death, envisioning this remembrance at the appropriate point in the service. Beyond these detailed stipulations governing prayers, scores of wills at least mention a 'Placebo, Dirige, and Requiem', or 'a mass of Our Lady', or a 'Trental of Gregory'.

As well as an interest in what prayers were said, there was a concern with who said them. Between the testator's intentions and their execution were many pitfalls. One of these was the failure of the hired clerical performers to do their job properly. We know that founders of chantries had a number of forms of legal recourse to employ against irresponsible priests, though the remedies did not always guarantee good service.[65] A less institutionalized way of purchasing quality was by asking that only men of exceptional probity be hired

[62] *TV*, p. 95.
[63] *TV*, p. 154.
[64] *TV*, p. 147.
[65] K. L. Wood-Legh: *Perpetual Chantries in Britain* (Cambridge, 1965), chapter 4.

Profundis, with the Lord's Prayer, the Angelical Salutation, and this prayer, "Deus cui proprium est miserere semper et parcere, propitia animae famuli tui Thomae, et omni ejus peccata dimitta, ut, mortis vinculis absolutus transire mereatur ad vitam." With these prayers also: "Inclina," and "Fidelium Deus, pro animabus parentum et progenitorum nostrorum inibi sepultorum." '

for the prayers in the first place. Just as 'the qualifications of the chantry priest are usually the vague requirements that the chaplain should be a fit person',[66] so many a noble in his will asked that the endowed masses be said 'by the most honest priest that can be found'.[67] That a special search had to be undertaken to turn up 'the most honest priest' may not speak well for the general level of available talent, but there is no indication that anyone refused to endow prayers just because he despaired of discovering men who were up to his standards. William Roos set his executors a hard task when he left order 'for the finding of ten honest chaplains'.[68] Some nobles were so particular as to want the priests to be 'kunning' as well as honest.[69]

The wills show us to what an extent the nobility not only absorbed the orthodox views of the church, but to what extent they constituted a group of co-operative participants. They received their values without much question from their church. Once educated and properly trained they actively and willingly took the role allotted them. They supported the system, and there is reason to think that they genuinely cared about it. The detailed prayer instructions are ample evidence that many laymen were versed in the liturgy, to the point of having opinions and preferences about services, hagiolatry, festivals, shrines, pilgrimages, relics, etc. The upper classes, if ignorant of Latin, did follow the services in their English primers, a not uncommon possession for people of substance.[70] If the liturgical preferences expressed in the wills indicate little about intellectual acumen or the depths of religious feelings, they at least indicate considerable superficial acquaintance with ecclesiastical routine. In a world where only the dissident few disputed that *enough of the right prayers* would help a soul through purgatory, there was room for considerable freedom of action when it came to choosing the right prayers.

The clergy may have welcomed this lay concern. They had little choice but to accept it if they sought endowments that were conditional on the right prayer services being said. Prayers for the dead were a good bargain, financially, and a sound investment spiritually as well. While some nobles preferred a large number of prayers to be

---

[66] *VCH Cambridge*, II, 152–3.
[67] *TV*, pp. 171, 175.
[68] *TV*, p. 182.
[69] *TV*, pp. 256, 265.
[70] Manning: *op. cit.*, p. 10.

said almost immediately after death,[71] others chose to have theirs spread out, usually at regular intervals, over a period of time which might run to the end of this world. But despite the immense variety of specifications, we can conclude that deathbed wishes were conservative in most instances, and were thoroughly expressive of the accepted values of the society. The nobles honoured the rules, which in turn helped exalt those who accepted and obeyed them.

[71] The feeling of an immediate need could be very strong. Lady West, *TV*, pp. 137–8: 'For four thousand and four hundred masses to be sung and said for the soul of Sir Thomas West, my Lord and husband, my own soul, and all Christian souls, in the most haste that may be, within 14 nights after my decease.' Also, *TV*, pp. 181, 208.

3

◇◇

Chantries

◇◇

THE chantry was the most popular, most widely endowed ecclesiastical institution of the later middle ages.[1] In a technical sense, chantries were 'provisions for daily or weekly masses and other services for a private intention, usually the repose of souls of particular individuals'. But here we speak of the chantry as a physical entity, the building, chapel, or altar at which such services were said. Dealing with the institution in this restricted sense is a necessity, for in the fuller context[2] 'Every form of pious benefaction, in fact, carried with it the obligation of intercession upon the beneficiary; and from this point of view every church, from the cathedral or abbey to the humble chapel of a remote hamlet, was a chantry foundation.' Chantries spread across the face of medieval England in a full diversity of grandeur, size, and legal variation. They eclipsed the older institutions of the church in popularity, and they competed successfully for the money of the patrons, founders, and benefactors, who in turn both helped create the new vogue and were swept along in it. The great men and great families of the realm built imposing chantry chapels and altars in the cathedrals, conventual churches, parish churches,[3] etc. They were both active and generous.

As we saw above, the nobles took the doctrines regarding the

[1] K. L. Wood-Legh: *Perpetual Chantries in Britain* (Cambridge, 1965), is now the basic study. There is still no survey of who founded chantries, or of how richly they endowed them.

[2] Thompson: *The English Clergy*, pp. 132–3. R. M. Clay: *The Medieval Hospitals of England* (London, 1966 reprint), pp. 29–30: 'All charitable foundations were to a certain extent chantries.'

[3] It seems that most parish churches of any size or substance were likely to have at least one chantry: *VCH Norfolk*, II, 242.

efficacy of prayers much to heart. They built new and splendid chantries; to their zeal we can attribute the imposing altars and tombs that we can still see in beautiful preservation at Ewelme, or in more skeletal form, as in the Hungerford chapel at Salisbury. On a lesser scale they endowed altars and bought the services of countless clerics. They revelled in the diversity of ecclesiastical forms permitted them, and they spread their endowments with both concern and pride. All branches of the church received their money, as well as the obligations imposed by the creation of a chantry.

Table 3 shows the recipients of the chantry endowments made by the nobles. The breakdown by percentage is on the basis of the number of grants made, rather than the number of different recipients

TABLE 3   Recipients of chantry grants, by years

Years	% to seculars	% to cathedrals	% to regulars	% to medicants	% to misc.	% no information	Total %	Total number
				Recipients				
1307–27	53	5	35	0	0	5	98*	17
1327–48	54	5	29	3	3	7	100	76
1348–77	43	11	31	2	9	4	100	54
1377–99	36	18	32	4	4	7	101	28
1399–1422	52	11	19	0	7	11	100	27
1422–60	56	12	14	4	6	8	100	50
1460–85	52	7	7	18	7	7	98	29

* Totals do not always equal 100 per cent because of rounding error.

(since one recipient might receive more than one grant). Furthermore, not every chantry for which an endowment was made, either by means of a licence to alienate or a bequest in a will, was necessarily ever set up. But, as we have said above, it is the intentions of the nobles that we investigate here.

Secular ecclesiastical recipients always received a very large proportion of the chantry endowments. Even their lowest share, 36 per cent of the grants made between 1377 and 1399, was above the share given to any other type of recipient, in any period. Their share was usually about 50 per cent of all the grants, and their total came to 140, of 281 separate endowments. But even counting the cathedrals as a separate category (disregarding the fact that some cathedrals were staffed by regulars and some by seculars), the number of potential secular recipients was many times that of the regular establishments. And in the period when grants to secular recipients was at its lowest, the cathedrals received their biggest share ever, 18 per cent of all the grants.

The regulars, including the mendicants, received about one grant in three all through the fourteenth century. But in the three periods in the fifteenth century, their cut fell to 19 per cent, 18 per cent, and 25 per cent (with the mendicants getting the bulk of this—five grants of seven given). This decline of popularity is in keeping with the general pattern of alienations. Since chantry endowments were one of the basic ways in which popular piety manifested itself, morally and economically, the regular orders may well have been aware of the crisis that confronted them. But of course, they did not meet as orders to receive an annual or decennial review of their economic statistics. Also, it is possible if improbable that there was a compensating increase in chantry endowments from other ranks of society. But the likelihood is simply that the monasteries were being ignored by those who sought to endow chantries, and that such houses were visibly both poorer and emptier as a result.

Some endowments and some chantries have doubtlessly escaped detection. The wills of the nobles reveal many chantry endowments not mentioned in the letters patent, and had we more wills, we would know of more chantries.[4] The wills are rather scarce before the reign of Richard II. Therefore for the early and mid-fourteenth century, generally a period of heavy endowment, one of our major sources is of limited value. Relying mostly on the patent rolls, we still find more creations and endowments made between 1327 and 1347 than in any other period. Thus the conclusions drawn in this chapter are based on incomplete evidence, and though there is little we can do besides recognize the lacuna, the problem remains with us throughout our inquiry.

Table 3 indicates a pattern of endowment which in quantitative terms is confirmed by data in later chapters. The greatest number of foundations and gifts occurred in the decades immediately preceding the plague, a lesser but still considerable number came in the later years of Edward III, and there was a continuing diminution in

---

[4] There is no way to determine how many alienations, once licences, were ever carried out, just as there is no key to the number of testamentary bequests not carried out: Jacob, pp. xxii-xxv.

Richard II's time. The early Lancastrian period saw the number of endowments hold at about the level of Richard's day, and then a decided increase took place again in Henry VI's reign. Through the entire two centuries the patent rolls would seem to be the prime source, but actually the fifteenth-century calendars provide almost no instances of relevant endowment, and the wills provide most of what information there is. By the 1420s more chantries were being set up and enriched through testamentary bequests (of cash and of personal possessions) than through the alienation of real property. It is possible, though unlikely, that property was being alienated in the fifteenth century without royal licence, and so knowledge of the transaction is lost. Lastly, under the Yorkist kings the endowments to chantries fall off once again in absolute numbers. There is little in this pattern to support the view that 'chantries were founded during the 14th, and *still more* frequently in the last half of the 15th century'.[5] The aristocracy may have played their most philanthropic tune earlier than other classes of lay benefactors, for by the second half of the fifteenth century the evidence is that their activity was becoming quite minimal.[6]

Through the entire period the nobles made 281 separate grants which were specifically designated for chantry purposes. This compares with the total of 446 licences to alienate in mortmain granted to them. Considering that the licences to alienate in mortmain might imply but little concern and an infinitesimal endowment, compared with the amount of money and interest that usually went into the endowment of a chantry (as shown in Table 4), the total of 281 grants is hardly a record of neglect or indifference. The average number of *per annum* chantry grants was 1·58. In the fourteenth century the average was 1·90, in the fifteenth century 1·20. Though this hardly seems magnificent as an annual rate of benefaction from the secular élite, a chantry could be founded and adequately endowed to stand through all eternity in one single action. The 281 grants went to about half that number of chantries. Coming as they did from some

[5] Capes: *op. cit.*, p. 271 (emphasis added). F. R. Raines (ed.): *A History of the Chantries within the County of Lancashire*, Chetham Society, old series, vol. lix (1862), and Wm. Page (ed.): *Yorkshire Chantry Surveys*, Surtees Society, xci (1894), for similar views.

[6] The wills of Londoners indicate that permanent chantries declined in endowments and popularity through the course of the fifteenth century. J. A. F. Thomson: 'Clergy and Laity in London, 1376–1531', Oxford D. Phil., 1960, pp. 212–15.

eighty-five different noble families, the endowments reflect a fairly widespread interest, both in terms of the total number of endowments and in their frequency.

Of the total, 62 per cent (or 175 grants) were made prior to 1399. These were scattered among various branches of the church, as were those made in the fifteenth century. Table 3 shows that exactly half of all the grants went to a chantry in a secular ecclesiastical establishment (not including the secular cathedrals). The recipient of these grants was usually a parish church, less frequently a secular college. The proportion of endowments received by secular institutions was about the same in each century: 83 of 175 grants in the fourteenth century, 57 of 106 in the fifteenth (47 per cent and 54 per cent respectively). If the popularity of chantries represented a manifestation of a general reaction against the regular orders, there was little momentum yet to be gained in this direction after the turn of the fourteenth century. Secular establishments were attracting pretty much the same proportion of the endowments in Edward IV's day as in Edward II's: 52 per cent in the 1460s and 1470s, 53 per cent in the early fourteenth century. Their share fell as low as 36 per cent in Richard II's time, but the cathedrals were the big gainers then, rather than the monasteries, and many cathedrals were secular institutions. But the reaction against the regulars, if that is what we are really seeing, must be kept in perspective. People may have built and endowed chantries because they no longer chose to found or to enlarge monasteries. But most chantries were smallish affairs anyway, built within existing houses of worship, and only the grandest of them can be considered as substitutes for the creation of *de novo* regular houses. We shall see that some nobles still did found regular houses.

The cathedrals received about one endowment in ten: 27 of 281. This was a larger share of spoils than they received from the licensed alienations. Alienations to cathedrals encompassed small bits of land, removed from the precincts of the church and representing accretions of wealth not readily visible to worshippers or visitors. In a great cathedral such a small grant would have been swallowed up among the benefactions of the centuries, and so perhaps even the greatest laymen of the land chose to alienate but little of their property to these giant foundations. But a chantry might be a different story. The size and splendour of the cathedral now might be an invitation, almost a challenge, to the spiritual ambitions of the peer. He built his chantry on an appropriate scale, in both the secular and regular cathedrals: Durham, Canterbury, Exeter, London, York, Norwich, Salisbury, Lincoln, Rochester, and Lichfield. Now the nobles were leaving monuments they could be proud of, complemented rather than eclipsed by the majesty of the cathedrals.

In the fifteenth century there was some movement away from the cloister as a host for the chantries, though again it is a story of relative neglect. Of the 68 chantry grants to regular houses, 54 (or 79 per cent of the total) were from the fourteenth century, and most of these (39 of 54) from Edward III's reign. Some of this is related to the connection between the desire to be buried in a church and the propensity to endow it, and will be treated below. But much of this popular 'alienation' from the monasteries and monasticism passes for what we call the temper of the times. Men were turning to the type of personally oriented religion exemplified by chantries, and they consciously turned their backs upon the older establishments. Either the religious orders did not compete for lay endowments, or they were singularly unsuccessful in attracting it in the face of competition from rival branches of the church. A few houses held their own, usually owing to extensive patronage from one great family. But for the most part neither the monasteries nor their monks could hope for significant enrichment through chantry endowments from the nobles. Their share of the grants fell sharply in the fifteenth century. They had received 37 per cent of the fourteenth century grants, but 13 per cent of those made after 1399.

The Austin Canons were the most popular regular order. Of the 56 grants going to monastic establishments, they attracted 32. This is without even including the grants to the completely new foundations at Maxstoke, Haltemprice, and Bisham, treated separately below. The Austins enjoyed most of their endowments in the fourteenth century, but they did play host to a new chantry as late as 1460, when the duke of Buckingham provided £100 for land to sustain a one-canon chantry at Maxstoke.[7] Endowments to other orders reflect the lack of interest among the laity. The Benedictines fared poorly, getting but thirteen grants, eight in the fourteenth century. Some of their great houses did come in for a single endowment: Faversham, Battle, Bury, Lewes, Evesham, etc. Four Cistercian and four Praemonstratensian houses received grants. Nunneries got but a few: one went to the Benedictine nuns at Cannington, and one to the Cister-

[7] *TV*, pp. 295–6.

cians at Greenfield.[8] Only one grant went to a Carthusian house, apart from the four new Charterhouses the nobles began. The friaries also did poorly, as they do not seem to have commended themselves for chantry purposes. However, this neglect is in contrast with their great popularity as shown in the wills. Together the Dominicans and the Franciscans shared eleven grants, a mere 4 per cent of those made.

Table 3 indicates the presence of a few miscellaneous grants. These mostly cover the few chantries set up in hospitals, which we might consider to be the ideal place for the melancholy business of praying, through all eternity, for the dead. There were no chantry endowments made to the universities, nor to any secular colleges, apart from the *de novo* foundations. But chantries were an institutionalized form of private spiritual succour, and it serves no useful purpose to view them in terms of social utility (except in so far as they served to employ masons, woodcarvers, and superfluous priests). Their social value was slight at best, and though much is made of their role in the history of education, the nobles have left little evidence of a deep concern with any aspects of the chantry other than the prayers it would provide in return for their money.

When they endowed a church for chantry services the nobles were usually generous enough. Though the terms of endowment are not always clear, where the amount of endowment is ascertainable it was at least £5 per annum in 82 per cent of the cases (124 of 152 grants), as shown in Table 4. This does not take into account the endowments with a value that cannot be assessed. An annual income of £5 was a reasonable one, and few priests could complain if they received their money promptly.[9] Half of the endowments returning £5 or more, per priest, were made in the fifteenth century. This is in keeping with a pattern we see elsewhere in this study—less quantitative activity in the fifteenth century, but what did go on was apt to be on a slightly more substantial scale. Another way of making this point is to say that in the fourteenth century 77 per cent of the chantry grants that can be

---

[8] Dugdale: *Baronage*, II, 11: the nuns received a grant for the continued support of an old chantry, dedicated in 1449 by Lord Welles to prayers for his ancestors.

[9] Wood-Legh: *Perpetual Chantries*, pp. 202–3: 'Chantries, like other benefices, varied considerably in value, though the differences between them were normally much less than those between rectories or even vicarages . . . From the mid-14th century onwards, however, few, if any, were established with annual revenues of less than six marks (four pounds) and most had at least seven marks, the amount with which an annualler was commanded to be content.'

analysed proved to be worth more than £5 per man, while in the fifteenth century the figure is 87 per cent. The letters patent refer to endowments of unspecified value, while the wills are more likely to detail the amount of annual subsidy. Since we rely on the letters patent more for fourteenth-century material, we know more about the size of the fifteenth-century grants: we can learn the value of 37 per cent of the fourteenth-century endowments and the value of 57 per cent of the fifteenth-century ones. However, only 28 of the 154 grants, or but 18 per cent of the total, are definitely stipulated as being worth less than £5 per annum per priest, and at no time period in the two centuries did the small endowments constitute more than one-third of the grants. These minimal endowments were usually in the form of small bits of land or tiny rents. Perhaps the grants found in the wills are larger because the imminence of death focused the donor's attention on the prayers soon to be said, and this would make him more likely to give lavishly for a chantry. The wills are distinctly more generous than are the letters patent.

TABLE 4   Value of grants to chantries, by years

		Value			
Years	% under £5	% over £5	% unknown value	Total %	Total number
1307–27	12	24	65	101*	17
1327–48	17	39	43	99	76
1348–77	6	33	61	100	54
1377–99	4	43	54	101	28
1399–1422	4	56	41	101	27
1422–60	6	56	38	100	50
1460–85	17	59	24	100	29

* Totals do not always equal 100 per cent because of rounding error.

The large grants were more than adequate. It is not surprising to find that the greatest laymen of the kingdom left endowments approaching £10 per priest, per annum. On the other hand they rarely exceeded this sum by much. The large chantry endowments, e.g., three appropriated advowsons, worth £40 13s 4d, or £20 in annual land and rent, or rents worth £106 13s 4d, went to chantries of more than one chaplain.[10] There was a practical limit to generosity, for an

[10] CPR 1348–50, p. 7; CPR 1350–54, p. 431; CPR 1391–96, p. 489.

endowment of much more than £10, if for a multi-chaplain chantry, would almost suffice to found an independent college, almshouse, or hospital. Why merely build an altar as an appendage to an existing foundation when for a little more one could become a founder, rather than simply a benefactor?

Many of the grants indicate how many priests were to be supported. The instances that can be identified are shown in Table 5. The services of a single chaplain were bought in 45 per cent of the cases (93 of the 209 grants which contain the information), and more than one officiating priest in 55 per cent of the cases. The ratio between one-man and multiple-chaplain chantries remains about the same through our period. Of the fourteenth-century grants, 45 per cent called for a single serving priest, as did 44 per cent of the fifteenth-century ones. Among all the chantries in England, one-man ones were undoubtedly more common, so in this regard, as perhaps in the average value of their endowments, the nobles were unusually generous. Only in the

TABLE 5   Stipulated size of chantries, by years

	Size				
Years	% one man	% more than one man	% no information	Total %	Total number
1307–27	47	29	24	100	17
1327–48	36	39	25	100	76
1348–77	22	17	61	100	54
1377–99	32	54	14	100	28
1399–1422	26	52	22	100	27
1422–60	30	50	20	100	50
1460–85	52	28	21	101*	29

* Totals do not always equal 100 per cent because of rounding error.

early fourteenth century and in the late fifteenth did they endow more one-man than multiple-priest chantries. They were extremely conspicuous in their consumption of spiritual goods.

While two priests were the common number in the multiple-chaplain establishments, more than two were not uncommon (Table 5). If Guy Beauchamp's ambitious provision of eight chaplains, in 1308, at Elmley Castle, may have proved abortive,[11] Lord Holland

[11] K & H, p. 329; CPR 1307–10, p. 136.

was not deterred two years later, and he obtained a licence to endow a chantry with a master and twelve chaplains.[12] If these large groups never became customary, for obvious reasons, they were not exotic rarities: two chaplains in a chantry in 1311, five in 1327, nine or ten in 1328, a master and twelve chaplains in 1438, seven in 1379 (in seven different places), five in 1394, ten honest chaplains in 1412, six in 1466 (in keeping with the provisions 'before determined'), etc.[13]

Obviously these large chantries rivalled many secular colleges in size and wealth. Manpower was no problem, judging from the provisions and from the comments of Wyclif and Langland, who claimed that founders hired chantry priests at the cost of stripping the realm of parish priests. Too many men, without the discipline of a collegiate or regular house, must have been difficult to control, and the large chantries were unwise investments. Neglect of duties, rather than gross immorality, may have been the usual result. Most of the chantries served by four or more men were within parish churches. Regular houses may have been reluctant to allow so many of their monks to be tied up for a special, extraneous purpose, even when the grant permitted the house to enlist new personnel to serve the chantry.

But some houses did accommodate the extravagant wishes of great patrons. The Franciscans at Canterbury housed a four-chaplain chantry, endowed to the value of 24 marks.[14] Five chaplains prayed in perpetuity within the Austin canonry at Campsey Ash for the soul of Maud Ufford.[15] Other cases can be found: one wonders how disruptive such activity was to regular life. Endowments for the support of chantries contributed but slightly to the over-all financial strength of a regular house. When the provision for a chantry was in a will which also contained an outright gift to that institution, the gift was mentioned as being separate from the chantry grant. The references in the letters patent are exclusively to the chantry, not for the general enrichment of the house. So while the priests who served the chantry thereby earned or supplemented their own income, the house which sheltered them did not necessarily profit. Honour and popularity might actually be a drain upon the institution, just as was the traditional obligation of hospitality.

[12] *CPR 1307–10*, p. 233.
[13] These are found, respectively, in: *Wills & Inventories*, p. 15; *CPR 1327–30*, pp. 137, 343; *CPR 1348–50*, p. 7; *TV*, pp. 104–5; *TE*, I, 202; *TV*, p. 182; *TV*, pp. 302–3.
[14] Gibbons, p. 6.
[15] *VCH Suffolk*, II, 113.

On the other hand a chantry utilizing priests already domiciled within an establishment may have relieved that house's financial burden. The more priests, the more altars, the more services; the greater the prestige of the house, and the greater chance of attracting more endowments. And so in the long run popularity could contribute to financial prosperity. Some endowments were explicitly labelled as being 'in augmentation' of the sustenance of a priest already in the house. This was likely to be an unqualified boon. But other grants were less considerate. Sometimes outsiders were to be brought in, to staff the chantry. These men might even be seculars. Or they might be men who only joined the order after they had been securely housed and employed in their new duties. Such lay interference and intrusion could hardly have helped the morale or the morals of a cloistered community. And yet the church could not readily refuse to say prayers, especially when they were adequately endowed prayers, subsidized by a family of some importance.

Most provisions of prayers stipulated that they were to be said forever. Some wills bequeathed vast sums to buy prayers at the funeral and immediately afterwards. These bequests are disregarded here, for such prayers were said by vast numbers of people, as soon as possible. The chantry, by way of contrast, implied a sort of sober regularization of prayers notably different from the deathbed attempt to launch the soul on its journey amid a veritable chorus. One year's worth of services was ordinarily the minimum duration for a chantry. Lady Welles was almost unique in asking for six months' worth of prayers, though she could not have really expected much more from a bequest of 36s 8d.[16] One year, three, five, seven, ten, or even twenty, or the rather quaint twenty winters,[17] for the life of the officiating priest, etc., are found in different wills and licences. While not all endowments were explicitly designed to ensure prayers in perpetuity, most of them were for something approaching that period, or to the 'end of the world', as Lucy Holland phrased the matter. Her nine priests, luxuriating in a bequest of 1,000 crowns, must have looked to the end of the world with equanimity.[18] The end of the world came, of course, with the suppression of the chantries in the 1540s. And this was only for those establishments which had been adequately

[16] *North Country Wills*, p. 55.
[17] *TV*, p. 226.
[18] *TV*, p. 205.

endowed, and were otherwise able to escape the vicissitudes which brought many chantries to a premature end.

If the endowment of a chantry was under £5 per annum, it was difficult to secure a priest on a permanent basis, unless the clerical supply exceeded the demand. This makes it probable that most grants of unknown quantity were above this, though a grant such as that of Henry Scrope, 'of six marks of rent', was unequivocal, if a bit meagre.[19] A few endowments were clearly on the light side. But most must be balanced towards generosity. Sometimes the adequacy of the grant is apparent from the sheer enumeration of its components: the alienation of a messuage, 20 acres of arable, 5 of meadow, 10 of pasture, and £1 rent would at least have come close to the standard.[20] Could two secular chaplains have been adequately supported from the income of 3 messuages, 3 tofts, a mill, 57 acres of land, 3 of meadow, and £1 14s 0d rent?[21] Since the donor was the ever-generous Elizabeth de Burgh, it would seem likely. She also endowed a single chaplain chantry with 7 messuages, 112 acres of arable, 8 of meadow, 10 of pasture, 10s 8½d rent, and the fair at Wynewall, Norfolk;[22] she was evidently accustomed to making grants of this type. But these miscellaneous endowments became less common in time. They were cumbersome, and the fluctuations of the land market undercut their value. This explains the fifteenth-century tendency to endow chantries with cash rents, reflected in the letters patent, rather than with a bit of arable land, and with lump sums of cash from personal treasuries, as illustrated in so many wills.

Though the proportion of chantry endowments in excess of £5 may have increased as we move from the fourteenth to the fifteenth century, there was no corresponding increase in the average size of the actual grants. And the increase in proportion of the total grants may be due to the shift from letters patent to wills as the major source. Any given nobleman was as likely to be generous in the early fourteenth century as in the late fifteenth. Endowments per priest did not change significantly through the course of the two centuries. Ralph Basset granted '100s. of rent issuing out of his manor of Drayton Basset to a chaplain to celebrate divine service daily' in 1319,[23] and in

---

[19] *CPR 1330–34*, p. 275.
[20] *CPR 1327–30*, p. 207.
[21] *CPR 1334–38*, p. 90.
[22] *Ibid.*, pp. 252–3.
[23] *CPR 1317–21*, p. 390.

1477 we find Margaret Beauchamp leaving £5 to the Dominicans at Worcester, that one priest might pray for her soul, for one year.[24] The fluctuations were from grant to grant, chantry to chantry, benefactor to benefactor. What we do find is that by the time of Henry VI the grants of foundation and endowment were becoming more complex. Fewer endowments were being made by means of patent letters, and quite a few were in concert with other donors, or in augmentation of earlier grants, or were guarded by the legal complications of incorporation. While many fifteenth century grants were in excess of £5, we can see that this was a standardized sum; we find a grant of £20 for four chaplains,[25] or, as provided by Lord Roos, of £400 for ten honest men for eight years' worth of prayers.[26] Lady Darcy was slightly below the standard wage when she left £200 to be divided among five chaplains for ten years. Maybe she thought the security she offered made the position attractive, even at only £4 per annum.[27]

The privileges of a founder or patron included giving directions regarding the personnel of the chantry. To order that outsiders be brought into a regular house to perform services might well have been a source of friction between patron and host. But it is a clue to the freedom of choice a benefactor could exercise. Nunneries had to accept this intrusion as they had to for their own liturgical needs, but the dearth of chantries located in nunneries indicate that this was a minor problem. However, when the Earl of March endowed the house at Wigmore so that the abbot would introduce 'two secular chaplains to celebrate divine service daily in their church', we begin to wonder how welcome the earl's beneficence was.[28] Richard Scrope endowed the Benedictine house at Richmond so that it would maintain ten additional regulars and two secular priests.[29] On the other hand, a house was always free to refuse a grant, and we do know of instances where a founder's terms were rejected.[30] Dictation bore a rather different complexion when Robert de Vere received licence 'to present two secular clerks to the said abbot for admission as monks, promotion to the priesthood, and appointment to the said chantry,

[24] Dugdale: *Baronage*, I, 250.
[25] PCC: Godyn, 10b (for 1454).
[26] Dugdale: *Baronage*, I, 552.
[27] *Repingdon*, p. 266.
[28] *CPR 1377–81*, p. 412.
[29] Dugdale: *Baronage*, I, 555.
[30] Wood-Legh: *op. cit.*, p. 145.

to fill up vacancies in this manner'.[31] Now the monastery was assured of a constant supply of pairs of men, plus the means of subsidizing them. But the overall picture reinforces our view of tension between the normal life of a regular house and the accommodations that had to be made when a chantry was erected.

Occasionally in the fourteenth century a chantry was founded physically apart from the regular house which got the endowment and which either staffed or supervised the staffing of the altar. If the endowment were a lavish one, the monastery might profit by employing a vicar. If not, using one of the monks would not help monastic discipline or stability. The constant services said by the chantry priest meant that unless the site were very near, constant travelling took place. Edmund Mortimer left Wigmore Abbey land for a two-chaplain chantry. The abbot was to find two secular priests, 'continually resident in the Church of Leintwardine, but not beneficed', to sing daily mass. They were to be presented to the bishop of Hereford, and then instituted to the chantry.[32] Gilbert Umfraville endowed the archdeacon of Lincoln so that the latter might provide chantry priests for him at the chapel of St Nicholas, Dokedyke.[33] None of these grants for 'external' chantries was so lavish that we can say with confidence that the houses were stretching orthodox practices just because of the financial inducement. The truth is more likely to be that there was nothing inherently offensive about the practice—a monastery was apt to be a responsible guardian of a spiritual trust. It was a permanent corporation, and its share of new benefactions depended in part upon its responsible administration of previous ones. If the house did not comply with his wishes, the patron could simply establish a chantry under the control of an independent secular priest. And if a patron wished to enrich a monastery for doing what he could have done on his own, the house would have been rather foolish not to accept his trust and his money. In an age of absentee control of both temporal possessions and eternal souls, external chantries were a minor matter. They emphasize the strength and the flexibility of the reciprocal ties between founder-patron and servant-priest.

[31] *CPR 1327–30*, p. 262.

[32] Dugdale: *Baronage*, I, 149.

[33] *CPR 1381–85*, p. 412. The Praemonstratensian houses at Titchfield, Hampshire and West Dereham, Norfolk, and the Benedictine house at Faversham, Kent, all accepted similarly directed endowments: *CPR 1330–34*, pp. 117–18; *CPR 1334–38*, pp. 252–3; *CPR 1307–13*, p. 159.

The geographical distribution of the chantry grants is much in keeping with the pattern for alienations in mortmain. Tied as they were to the generosity of the great families, chantries were bunched wherever an expansive clan concentrated its philanthropy. No alienations in mortmain were licensed for the corners of England— Cornwall, Chester, Westmorland. This was likewise true for chantry grants. There was one endowment to a Lancashire chantry, to the church at Manchester, later converted into Manchester College by Lord de la Warre. No grants were made in Dorset, or in Cumberland (except the *de novo* foundation of Greystoke College), and only two in Durham. Though the Percys and Nevilles held sway there, they preferred to rest forever and to be remembered elsewhere, particularly in Yorkshire. The west country drew a fair share of attention, and thanks largely to the families of Hungerford, Beauchamp, and Berkeley there were fifteen grants in Somerset, four in Devon, seventeen in Wiltshire, nine in Worcester, eight in Warwickshire, four in Gloucester, and nine in Salop and in Herefordshire, thanks mostly to the Mortimers.

London establishments fared well. The prestige attached to founding a chantry helped attract money from peers who had no other London connections. Some of the religious houses there were popular burial grounds for nobles; the life to come was frequently associated with life in London. The Blackfriars received 10 marks for a one-year chantry, from Lord Scrope, a Yorkshire magnate.[34] They also had a chapel for the Tiptofts, earls of Worcester, in their church.[35] As well as other chantries at the Blackfriars, the nobles endowed chantries at Holy Trinity without Aldgate, endowed with 1,000 crowns: St Katherine near the Tower, endowed to the tune of 12 marks per annum for each of the four performing clerks: the hospital of St Thomas Acon, and the London Austin friary.[36] Several chantries were endowed at St Paul's,[37] and Marie de St Pol established a chantry for Aymer de Valence at Westminster Abbey.[38] Most London

[34] *TE*, III, 298.

[35] *VCH London*, I, 500.

[36] For these four chantries, respectively: *TV*, p. 205; *RW*, p. 283; *VCH London*, I, 493, and I, 510.

[37] The total number of chantries in St Paul's has been estimated to be between 35 (served by 54 priests) and 47: Raines: *op. cit.*, p. xiv.

[38] Aymer was buried immediately north of the high altar, for the best view of royal ceremonies possible. But he almost lost his place to General Wolfe, 'a proposal averted by the better sense of Horace Walpole'. A. P. Stanley: *Historical Memorials of Westminster Abbey* (New York, 1888), II, 90.

chantries were endowed with cash, but those financed by alienated land drew their sustenance from property within the city. Lord Fanhope granted the Preaching Friars 40 marks rent from London real property holdings,[39] and others tapped the same source for pay for the prayers they ordered said.

The counties around London drew but few grants: Surrey got two, Bedfordshire two, Buckinghamshire two, Hertfordshire none at all. Twelve grants went to Kent, but mostly away from the London area, as with the alienations in mortmain. Endowments went to establishments in Canterbury, Faversham, Rochester, etc.; only one chantry was endowed as near the city as Greenwich. In Essex and Berkshire this was also the case, for the nine and ten grants which they attracted respectively were far from the dormitory areas. The Midlands were thinly endowed: two grants in Nottingham, four in Derby, five in Oxfordshire, five in Leicester, five in Staffordshire. Sussex, with three grants, and Hampshire with four were about equally popular, though the Sussex figure does not include the Fitz-Alan foundations at Arundel. East Anglia reflects more activity, and there were eleven chantry endowments in Suffolk, ten in Norfolk, four in Cambridge. But Lincolnshire and Yorkshire were the centres of most beneficence: 22 grants were made to Lincoln chantries, 37 to those of York.

While grants were usually made to but a single institution, a patron might name a number of places at which his chantries were to be placed. These multiple-chantry endowments owed their existence to the generosity or impetuosity of donors in a hurry, and most such endowments come in the wills. One form of patronage was the creation of two chantries, each staffed by its own priest, with a variant being the use of two men in one place, and a third man elsewhere.[40] Lady Bergavenny endowed two priests to sing for her in the parish church at Rochford, and three at Kirkby Bellers.[41] We also find a provision for four chaplains to celebrate in three places: the simultaneous creation of nine chantries, seven of them in London, all from the same grant: the endowments of a year's worth of prayers at seven places, etc.[42] There are also endowments made at different times which add personnel to a going institution. Cash residues, after

[39] *CPR 1436–41*, pp. 55–6.
[40] *CPR 1345–48*, p. 434; *CPR 1330–34*, p. 103.
[41] *Jacob*, p. 536.
[42] *TV*, pp. 126, 205, and 104.

debts and bequests were paid, usually went for large clusters of prayers to be said quickly, rather than to chantries. Usually the multiple-chaplain chantries located in secular houses were composed of a group of priests of equal status. They shared the joint or common income, and were not independently supported from lands and rents, as were canons in a prebendal system. The priests duplicated each others' functions. But volume, rather than diversity of prayer services, was at a premium. Whatever problems arose from these crowded and unstructured chantries did not become so serious that the practice of creating and endowing them came to an end. Instances of the overstaffed chantry are found in both centuries. The knowledge that they had a common self-interest must have served to keep groups of from two to twelve men together in some harmony.

The presence of such a contingent, free from ordinary parochial duties and serving a private religious interest, must have been an irritant to the parish priest,[43] excluded as he was from the income of the chantry. But though this practice seemed in obvious need of reform, it lasted as long as the chantries themselves. Sometimes the chantry was located in a parish church, under the direct patronage and supervision of the founder of the chantry or his family. This would have minimized any discontent due to the chantry's presence, as it would have continuously re-emphasized the extent to which local spiritual life depended on the largesse of the local magnate.[44]

When the chantry was within the confines of a regular house, the head of that establishment accepted some responsibility for its upkeep. This responsibility, qualified by the instructions of the lay founder, extended to cover priests praying elsewhere but supported by an endowment given to the house (as the vicar was answerable to the institution holding the appropriation of the advowson). The burden on the abbot was correspondingly increased when more than one chantry chaplain had to be supervised.[45] But chantry priests were placed within a tightly structured situation in only a few instances.

[43] Legislation was passed to steer priests into pastoral positions, with only the surplus manpower to serve in chantries. But the legislation was ineffective: McKisack: *op. cit.*, p. 304.

[44] There are numerous examples of the strength of local ties: Basset at Drayton, *CPR 1334–38*, pp. 301, 549; Mortimer at Lentwardine, *CPR 1327–30*, p. 343; Zouche at Weston in Arden, *CPR 1343–45*, p. 455; Courtenay at Colcombe, *CPR 1343–45*, p. 431; Roos at Belvoir, Dugdale: *Baronage*, I, 552.

[45] Patrons subsidized anything from two priests (in Salisbury cathedral), *CPR 1467–77*, p. 306, to the thirteen seculars put in the charge of the abbot of Campsey Abbey: Dugdale: *Baronage*, II, 49.

Grants frequently refer to a group of chaplains, organized under one of their number who was to be designated as their master or warden.[46] He would preside over as many as '12 other chaplains'.[47] The warden of a chantry might be authorized to receive new endowments, perhaps to support additional priests, whom he was now to find.[48] William Latimer paid the master of the chantry at Helping 20 marks per year, while his other twelve chaplains only received half that amount.[49]

Not until the fifteenth century did the nobles set up chantries which were incorporated, explicitly, and were 'capable of acquiring lands and other possessions and of pleading and of being impleaded in any court'.[50] As a corporation the chantry, usually but not necessarily of more than one chaplain, was now 'able to appropriate in mortmain lands, rents, and possessions, to the value' named in the licence.[51] The whole subject of the chantry as a corporation has recently been treated,[52] and the material on such foundations of the nobles sheds little light on the subject. One licence enjoining incorporation carried the provision that if the chantry were not set up as directed, the dean of Lincoln was to get the alienated advowson and to endow the two chantry chaplains himself by means of the property bestowed upon him.[53] But only some half dozen of the licences to alienate specifically mention incorporation, as does one single will.

The grants of foundation and endowment do not usually carry many details concerning the actual building or the ultimate appearance of the completed chantry. But from the occasional use of a phrase such as 'according to the tenor of a certain indenture made between the said convent and myself',[54] we can see that benefactors had entered into the details of a foundation, perhaps years before the actual moment of enrichment. Lord Vescy's will provided money for six chantries, 'in such places as I have before determined'.[55] A letter patent which permitted the creation of a chantry concluded with 'as

[46] *CPR 1345–48*, p. 12: '. . . to find two chaplains, whereof one shall be the principal one.' No criterion is given for distinguishing the man to be designated as master.
[47] *CPR 1377–81*, p. 32; *CPR 1348–50*, p. 7.
[48] *CPR 1338–40*, p. 25.
[49] *CPL 1362–1404*, p. 91.
[50] *CPR 1446–52*, p. 557.
[51] *CPR 1441–46*, p. 453.
[52] Wood-Legh, *op. cit.*, pp. 315–30.
[53] *CPR 1436–41*, p. 137.
[54] *TV*, p. 246.
[55] *TV*, pp. 302–3.

he shall ordain': only one indication of a continuing concern and a series of negotiations between him who paid and him who was to pray.[56] A few peers stipulated that their new foundations were to bear specific names: sometimes a non-personal one, such as the chantry 'to be called the chantry of St George' or 'to be called the chantry of St Mary, Alnwick', or 'the chantry of the blessed apostles Peter and Paul of Hacconby'.[57] Other men were less reticent, and spoke of the day when there would stand 'the chantry to be called the chantry of the Earl of Salisbury of Chesterfield', or 'Therle of Warrewyk chaunteries', or 'said chantry to be called "Phelippes chaunteries of Denyngton" '.[58] The priest might be singled out as 'a chaplain of the Viscount's "chantery" ', etc.[59] All of these named chantries were mid-fifteenth-century creations, when the declining number of creations was countered by the increased size of the new foundations and a greater sense of identification and of possessiveness on the part of the founders. Popular religion and patronage were becoming even more personalized than previously.

Chantries were an individualized form of institutionalized religion. While men of lesser rank and resources might join gilds and fraternities for collectively endowed prayers, the nobles usually had their own altars. Family feeling, not corporate activity, built and maintained their chantries. Almost never does a peer make an endowment to a chantry not built by a direct ancestor or close relation. Their proprietorial instincts are borne out here, as they are when we look at their *de novo* foundations. They were only too willing to keep hands off each other's projects, and the resulting proliferation of chantries was certainly pleasing to the recipients. But all the noble endowments together only enriched a small fraction of the churches, cathedrals, monastic houses, and other would-be beneficiaries. Like the professional legacy seekers of Jacobean comedy, a great deal of the late medieval church lived on expectations and hopes. One wonders what sort of terms competing clerics offered to rich laymen to catch their attention.

Any discussion of the activities of different families must be qualified by a recognition of the inequalities within the ranks of the

---

[56] *CPR 1343–45*, p. 438.
[57] *CPR 1467–77*, p. 90; *CPR 1446–52*, p. 170; *CPR 1441–46* p. 41.
[58] *CPR 1441–46*, p. 453; *CPR 1461–67*, p. 462; *CPR 1436–4* ,p. 78.
[59] *CPR 1441–46*, p. 41.

nobility. We cannot fairly disparage a minor clan by comparing it with the Beauchamps, Nevilles, or Percys. Vast gradations of wealth, prestige, and territorial control existed under the rubric of noble. On the other hand, we know that bald economic and political factors are not invariably a guide to philanthropic activity. Strong local partisanship or the impetus provided by one munificent lord might suffice to reverse any pattern which wealth and political position would lead us to expect. Genuine religious feeling cannot be totally discounted, hard though it might be to measure, and rarely though we can be sure of its existence. Other motives—jealousy, the desire to imitate, promises rashly made but honoured nevertheless—cannot be ignored, and their tangible results can be tallied. Family tradition was a strong motive force. All the families studied here had adequate resources so that, with sufficient incentive, even the least of them could compare well with the greatest.

About 85 different noble families made the 281 chantry grants, but only four made more than ten separate grants. These four, Neville, Hungerford, Beauchamp, and Berkeley, made 68 grants between them, or about 25 per cent of the total. Ten more families made six or more; a total of 75 grants came from these ten, or 27 per cent of the total. Thus 14 different families (16 per cent of the families) made 143 grants, or 51 per cent of the total. The top of this steep pyramid contained mostly families of major import, e.g. Stafford, de la Pole, Holland, Percy, Montague, and Mortimer, in addition to those already cited. But the presence of the Hungerfords and the Berkeleys at the top is testimony to the way in which relatively minor noble families, with strong incentive and local prestige, could carve out a major position for themselves in the realm of ecclesiastical benefaction. The families of Basset, Roos, Scrope, and Willoughby all made over six grants. These names also reflect families with strong local preoccupation. But in a sense so does every chantry endowment. Most grants were either in cash or in property located near the foundation, so from the geographical point of view almost all grants were made by a local lord, even if the chantry were far from his major home. Eleven families made 4 or 5 grants, 21 families but 2 or 3. Among these 32 families making a small number of endowments—though we must remember that the number of grants has no correlation with the size of the grant—we find the names of Courtenay, de Vere, Fitz-Alan (without benefit here of their own *de novo* foundations), Despenser, Ufford, and Beaufort. Thirty-nine families made but a single grant: 46 per cent of the families therefore contributed but 14 per cent of the grants.

Most of the instances of benefaction were from the fourteenth century: 175 of the 281, or some 62 per cent of the total. Of the 85 families involved, 61 made grants in the fourteenth century, 55 in the fifteenth. If we separate them by their activity in the two centuries and count them as 116 different families, we find that 52 per cent of the families (61 of 116) made 62 per cent of all the grants in the fourteenth century. This means that fourteenth-century activity was not only greater in absolute numbers, but in the relative one of grants per family. There was a greater average value to the fifteenth-century grant, but this was only slight, and we cannot explain away the declining number of fifteenth-century grants wholly in terms of there then being fewer families among the nobility. After 1399 each family was making proportionately fewer endowments to chantries. However, the breakdown by centuries is artificial. The Berkeleys made 23 of their 24 grants in the fourteenth century, when they also received most of their licences to alienate. The Montagues made seven of their nine grants in the fourteenth century, the Percys six of their seven (though their licences to alienate were about evenly divided). The fifteenth-century total in turn is boosted by some active families not in the fourteenth-century peerage, e.g. the Hungerfords, with fifteen grants, the de la Poles with seven (and none from the late fourteenth century). The Nevilles evenly divided their fourteen grants, the Beauchamps gave nine of fifteen in the latter century. Some trends emerge, but it is hard to be certain about many specific cases.

This survey has stressed that chantries were an element of private, individualized (or familial) religion in an age when most worship was public and collective. But we recognize that what was individualistic was also selfish. This censure is reinforced when we note that only the barest handful of chantry grants carried any charitable provisions. Not that the nobles did not give to the poor. But when their thoughts turned towards their own chantries, they usually had no mind for eleemosynary considerations. They cared about themselves at that critical moment. Their chantries were not often linked to the creation of a national school system.[60] Their egocentrism only admits

[60] The chantry of the Percys at Cockermouth was licensed to conduct classes, while the grammar school founded by Lady Katherine Berkeley at Wotton under Edge in 1384 was independent of any chantry foundation: A. F. Leach: *The Schools of Medieval England* (London, 1915), pp. 208, 211.

of a few exceptions. John Warrenne's grant of land to the Dominicans at Thetford was for a two-chaplain chantry and for 'food and hospitality for 13 poor persons at a certain time of the year, and to do divers others works of piety there established'.[61] The earl of Warwick's grant to the monastery at Evesham was to provide for alms and other pious works, in addition to prayer services.[62] One of the chaplains in the chantry Henry Percy founded in 1448 was also 'to teach poor boys grammar without payment, and to do other works of piety'.[63] But this handful is about the extent of endowments to chantries which also indicated any concern for others than the founder, his kin, and some immediate friends. The small number of these grants is eloquent testimony to the exclusiveness and selfishness of chantry-religion.

Miss Wood-Legh has intimated that chantries helped prepare the way for the religious changes of the sixteenth century because they offered a scope for individual expressions of religious sentiment and because they emphasized lay control of priests and priestly functions.[64] These views seem eminently correct. But, for the nobles at least, the surprise is not that the chantry led toward the future but rather that it brought out no greater individualism, no greater sense of self-awareness in the later middle ages. Most noble families engaged in church building. But they did so with a complete obeisance to customary behaviour, being slightly on the generous side of average, being slightly crabby about special conditions, and showing no unwillingness to perpetuate the system indefinitely. If any nobles (except a few who flirted with Lollardy) felt any restiveness, it was manifested in a negative fashion—by not making grants to chantries. Otherwise, the traditional forms of popular religion seemingly satisfied our élite group. Perhaps they owed their political and economic dominance in no small part to the fact that, in other realms of behaviour and activity, they blended so nicely with their followers. As a class they had little interest in questioning the values of their world order or in making radical changes in the established relationships between the laity and the church.

[61] *CPR 1334–38*, p. 158.
[62] *CPR 1348–50*, p. 565.
[63] *CPR 1446–52*, p. 170.
[64] Wood-Legh: *op. cit.*, p. 314.

4

<hr />

New foundations

<hr />

BEHIND the foundation of any ecclesiastical institution lay the support of a layman. Often the very idea and the moving force was his, as well as the bulk of the money which raised the stones and fed the monks, canons, or priests and inmates. The contributions of the nobles toward this most personal and most expensive form of ecclesiastical benefaction, the building of *de novo* foundations, were not inconsiderable. Even in the fourteenth and fifteenth centuries, when the glorious days of new creations were largely over, the nobles still gave handsomely to build new establishments, both large and small.

Table 6 tells the story in brief. Disregarding the distinction between various orders and between regular and secular houses, there were about thirty distinctly new foundations which owed their existence to the generosity of a nobleman. Several others, though not included in the total because of special problems, at least merit passing attention. Of the thirty or so new institutions, fourteen were regular houses, including five for the mendicants, while twenty were secular: nine hospitals, nine colleges, and two academic (university) colleges. This building activity came despite the fact that 'the popularity of all (religious orders) undoubtedly fell considerably between 1350 and 1360, and ... new foundations after 1350 of all the monks and canons, black and white, and of friars of all kinds, are less than twenty in number all told'.[1] Eight of the fourteen regular foundations begun by the nobles come after 1350 (though one, the Franciscan house at Ware, came in 1351).

Why did the nobles show so well in this regard? They were wealthy,

[1] K & H, p. 48.

TABLE 6   New foundations

Order	House	Founder	Date	1535 net income £	Known details
Benedictine	Upholland, Lancs.	Holland	1319	53	Secular College, 1310–19
Carthusian	Kingston, Yorks. (Hull)	de la Pole	1377	174	Originally Franciscan nuns
	Coventry	de la Zouche	1381	131	
	Axholme, Lincs.	Mowbray	1397–8	237	
	Mountgrace, York	Holland	1398	323	
Austin Canons	Haltemprice, Yorks.	Wake	1325–6	100	Founded 1322 at Cottingham
	Bisham, Berks.	Montague	1337	185	
	Maxstoke, War.	Clinton	1337	81	Sec. Coll., 1331
	Flanesford, Here.	Talbot	1346	14	
	(Badlesmere, Kent)	Badlesmere	1320		(Probably abortive)
Franciscans	Walsingham, Norf.	Eliz. de Burgh	1347		
	Ware, Herts.	Wake	1351		
	Aylesbury, Bucks.	Butler	1387		
Austin Friars	Atherstone, War.	Basset	1375		
Franciscan Nuns	Denney, Camb.	St Pol	1342	172	Moved from Waterbeach
Hospital	Well, Yorks.	Neville	1342	42	
	Hull, Yorks.	de la Pole	1376–7		Inc. with Charterhouse
	Arundel, Sussex	FitzAlan	1380		
	(Donnington, Berks.)	de la Pole	1393		
	Brackley, Northants.	Lovell	1423		
	Ewelme, Oxon.	de la Pole	1437	64	
	(Abingdon, Berks.)	de la Pole	1442		Several founders
	Heytesbury, Wilts.	Hungerford	1449		
	(Thame, Oxon.)	de la Pole	1460		Several founders
	Alkmonton, Derby	Blount	1474		12th c. house, refounded
Colleges	Astley, War.	Astley	1343	39	Chantry founded, 1338
	Cobham, Kent	Cobham	1362	128	Founded as chantry
	Arundel, Sussex	FitzAlan	1380	168	
	Greystoke, Cumb.	Greystoke	1382	82	
	Staindrop, Durham	Neville	1408	126	With alms-house
	Stoke-by-Clare, Suff.	Mortimer	1415–19	324	Alien. Ben. house converted
	Manchester	de la Warre	1421	213	
	Tattershall, Lincs.	Cromwell	1439–40	348	
	St William, York	Neville	1455	22	
	(Elmley, Worcs.)	Beauchamp	1308–41	55	Inadequate endowment
	(Ruthin, Denb.)	Grey of Ruthin	1310		
	(Spilsby, Lincs.)	Willoughby	1347	40	
	(North Cadbury, Som.)	Botreaux	1423	28	
	(Lingfield, Surrey)	Cobham	1431	75	
Academic Colleges	Clare Hall, Camb.	Burgh	1326–46	84	
	Pembroke Hall, Camb.	St Pol	1347	153	
	(Buckingham Coll., Camb.)	Stafford	15th c.		

far beyond most of their fellows of course. While it did not take a fortune to build a *de novo* foundation, it at least required the willingness to part with several hundred pounds. The nobility were apt to be religiously conservative, for the most part, and the creation of new foundations was an old approach to religious enthusiasm. All such an institution needed was a single peer, acting perhaps with and

New foundations

sometimes without the acquiescence of his family. The money and the desire could still be found in the later middle ages. Added to the general veneration of tradition, we should recall the role a peer played in his local empire. His local role often called upon him to act in a style that his national importance never justified.

None of the regular foundations was begun after 1398.[2] Nor was a regular house to be found among the fifteenth-century foundations. All those which the nobles founded in our period came in the generation or two immediately after the Black Death. After 1400 their exclusive concern was with secular establishments, which they continued to found through the century. Perhaps for the peers 1399 was a turning point of significance in realms other than politics. Eleven of their twenty new secular houses came in the fifteenth century. The nine fourteenth-century ones included three of their nine new hospitals, four colleges, and both the academic foundations. Only four of the nine fourteenth-century institutions antedated 1350 (including both Cambridge colleges). So the picture is one showing a diversion of interest from the regular to the secular branches of the church by the fifteenth century. There was almost no noble interest in the universities in the fifteenth century; very little endowment, let alone new foundations. Nor was there anything closer to London than Thame, Ewelme, and Stoke-by-Clare. Of the thirty-four creations, twelve were in the north (including Lincoln), and six were in Yorkshire alone. The large cities were generally avoided in the fifteenth century, even more than in the fourteenth.

A few generalizations can be ventured. Old sites were often sought out for new foundations. Frequently the grounds of an older house, now dissolved or decayed, were selected for a new effort. The reasons were partially physical; the presence of buildings or building materials, and sometimes the local concentration of revenue-producing lands and possessions. But also, local traditions associated certain places with religious usage. Consecrated ground exercised a peculiar and lasting fascination. The strength of the call to pilgrimage is a

---

[2] The commitment, on the part of the Hollands, towards the creation of a Benedictine House at Upholland, Lancashire, was so minimal as to scarcely warrant mention. A secular college had been founded in 1310, but the canons 'had been quarrelsome and worship had been neglected': (*Monasticon*, IV, 409), and the house was converted to a priory of Black Monks in 1319. The value of the house, in 1535, was only £53 3s 4d, and it seems safe to say that it was an insignificant establishment. There is no record of any endowments from the Holland family.

reminder of how seriously a place could be esteemed in popular religion apart from the buildings on it.

The nobles often showed a singular lack of resolution when they went to found a house. If we think of the ruthlessness of Wolsey at Magdalen College we badly miss the approach of many lay founders.[3] Many establishments grew from a small beginning, often as a chantry, by means of a number of gradual steps. The patron only slowly became so enthusiastic that he finally committed himself to his new project in a serious way. This is apart from several foundations which moved to the new site after their first creation. The pattern of endowment followed by most founders, even the most generous, was gradually to build the wealth of the house through a number of grants. Few gave so much in the original endowment that the house was able to stand on its own legs from birth. Uncertainty at the beginnings of the project might encompass the location, the type of institution, its wealth and size. The pressures on a founder to enlarge his own creation were strong, and worked against the tendency to regret one's enthusiasm and to try to retrench.

Few nobles were content simply to give money and then to allow the house to go its own way. Most of the statutes we have, particularly for hospitals and colleges, show the founder's concern with the spiritual welfare of the inmates and with the moral and even the intellectual climate of the house. The regular houses were more uniformly controlled by their order, and accordingly there was less scope for lay domination. This disputed domination may help explain their lack of popularity. The new foundations were built for the glory of God and the souls of the founder, his relatives and friends. To him the house was a form of super-chantry.[4] No wonder he was concerned with the state of life of those who would offer the prayers. They were not only supported by his largesse, but in turn would exert some control over his immortal soul. The founder's proprietorial interference is a general rule of philanthropic activity. The man of property is concerned with the wisdom and risk of

[3] There were numerous abortive foundations. Such a list would include the Percy College at Exham, Northumberland (*CPR 1452-61*, p. 218), for which elaborate rules and guidelines were proposed. There was to have been a Bonshommes House, built by Lord Grey of Ruthin, in 1478: R. I. Jack: 'The Lords Grey of Ruthin', London Ph.D., 1961, pp. 113, 138; and a college of thirteen chaplains, which William Latimer intended to found at Helpringham (*CPL 1362-1404*, p. 91, and *GEC, s.n.*).
[4] H. M. Colvin: *The White Canons in England* (Oxford, 1959), pp. 262-6.

his ventures, and he demands the appropriate return. Benefactions were only half of a reciprocity—both sides accepted this and approached the exchange accordingly. So the patron called the tune about conditions and rules; his directions did not end at the monastic gatehouse.

Most foundations were basically the end product of one man's attention, perhaps supplemented by bequests from other members of his family. The peers did not often touch each other's favourite ecclesiastical concerns, and the tradition was that one family took care of a particular house.[5] The details of the establishments covered here are mostly limited to the endowments of the founder and his family, though in a few instances where another peer contributed, it has been duly noted. The narratives below are not histories of the houses. Rather, they are intended to indicate how a medieval founder went about building up his foundations. No generalization can be made as to the amount of money, the length of time, or the depth of interest needed for a *de novo* creation. As they stood at the pinnacle of ecclesiastical benefaction, so the ranks of founders is necessarily small. That the de la Poles were involved in the creation of a Charterhouse and no fewer than four hospitals is perhaps as much evidence of the way in which they sought to buy their way into the front ranks of the peerage, as it is of their wealth, import, and piety. The FitzAlans, the Beauchamps, and the Nevilles were active in rough proportion to their prominence. But names we might well expect to find, for example, Percy, Beaufort, Berkeley, are absent, while such minor ones as Clinton, Wake, and Astley figure in the tale. Foundation, in the last analysis, was a thing so personal that a man's character and desires must tell the final story.

Of the nine Carthusian houses in England at the Reformation, six were begun after 1350, and four of these by nobles, while one more was a royal foundation.[6] The de la Pole foundation at Kingston-upon-Hull was a house of only moderate size and wealth. On the other hand the family had a sustained interest in the religious life of their native Hull, and other foundations of theirs are treated below. In 1377 the king permitted Michael de la Pole to endow a new Charterhouse with property to the yearly value of 200 marks.[7]

[5] For a different view of social interaction, see S. Painter: 'The Family and the Feudal System in 12th Century England', *Speculum*, XXXV (1960), pp. 11–12.

[6] D. Knowles: *The Religious Orders in England*, II, pp. 129–30, and E. M. Thompson: *The Carthusian Order in England* (London, 1930).

[7] *Ibid.*, pp. 201–4.

Grants in 1379 satisfied £100 of this.[8] The Carthusians claimed that they had lost out 'on account of the judgement against him (Michael) in Parliament',[9] and so another alienation was permitted in 1398, this time for bits of land with an aggregate value of a mere £1 18s 4d.[10] In 1436 William de la Pole alienated land 'worth 40s a year, in satisfaction of six marks a year of the £20 yearly of land and rent' originally permitted.[11] He gave the house land 'as of the value of £10 yearly . . . in part satisfaction of the tenements and advowsons to the value of 200 marks granted by letter patent of Edward (III)'.[12] Michael asked to be buried there, if he died in the north,[13] and William requested both burial and commemoration by means of a stone image for himself and his wife, and daily masses.[14] Other northern families showed a willingness to support the house, despite its strong ties with a particular and not overly popular family. John Neville endowed prayers there.[15] Richard Scrope left the Carthusians 10 marks,[16] and John Scrope of Masham left £20, 'proemendacione unius finis elevati'.[17]

The least of the noble Charterhouses was that at Coventry, founded by Lord Zouche of Harringworth. He received a licence in 1381 to found the house and to dedicate it to St Anne. He left it 14 acres of land, and asked his heirs to endow it with property returning an annual income of 100 marks. But on his death the work was taken up by the citizens of Coventry, rather than by the founder's own kin, and the house passes from our view. The king was an active patron, but the only other noble with any affiliations was the earl of Warwick,[18] who built one of the cells attached to the Charterhouse.[19]

Thomas Mowbray, earl of Nottingham, founded the house at Axholme in Lincolnshire in 1395 or 1396.[20] A letter patent licensed him to found, and to alienate 100 acres, and to bestow upon the

---

[8] *CPR 1377–81*, p. 318. In 1383 another £13 12s 4d worth of land was alienated, in satisfaction of the same licence: *CPR 1381–85*, pp. 305–6.

[9] *CPR 1391–96*, p. 368.

[10] *CPR 1396–99*, p. 464.

[11] *CPR 1429–36*, p. 599.

[12] *CPR 1436–41*, p. 498.

[13] Jacob, p. 59.

[14] *North Country Wills*, p. 51.

[15] *Wills and Inventories*, II, 40.

[16] *TE*, I, 274.

[17] *TE*, I, 339.

[18] *VCH. Warwick*, II, 83; E. M. Thompson: *op. cit.*, pp. 208–9.

[19] Dugdale: *Baronage*, I, 237.

[20] *VCH. Lincoln*, II, 158. K & H, p. 122, where it is given as 1397 or 1398.

new house the alien priory of Monkskirby, a foundation of his ancestors.[21] He had pressured the church for a decade for permission to divert the revenues of this old and decayed house for a more vital use.[22] Monkskirby was worth about £200 a year, though Axholme did not finally get clear title to the income until 1414.[23] In addition to land, the earl followed up his foundation gift with a rental worth 29 marks yearly, miscellaneous perquisites, and the advowsons of the churches at Epworth and Belton. A house was established for a prior and twelve monks. The Mowbrays later contributed 'a tun or two pipes Gascon wine from the King's wines in Kingston-upon-Hull in aid of maintenance and celebration of masses' in 1415,[24] and the advowson of Silby church, worth 14 marks per annum, in 1447.[25] John Mowbray asked for burial there,[26] and Thomas Mowbray wanted to have his father's bones brought home from Venice and placed in Axholme, next to his own.[27]

The last Charterhouse founded by a noble was at Mountgrace, Yorkshire. Thomas Holland began the project in 1396. He obtained possession of the alien priories of Hinckley, Wareham, and Carisbrooke—all attached to St Mary Lyre in Normandy—for the Mountgrace foundation.[28] The king, out of great love for his nephew (as we are told), ratified this substantial endowment and then licensed a further alienation, the manor of Bordelby.[29] The founder was reburied in his house in 1411,[30] though it was not completed until 1440. Thomas Beaufort left £40 and a silver cross to the monks.[31] However, the bulk of the endowments which made the house so wealthy and large—there were 21 monks in 1535—came from the founder.[32]

We know that the Austin Canons were popular among the nobles.

[21] *CPR 1391–96*, p. 607.
[22] *VCH. Lincoln*, II, 158.
[23] K & H, p. 87.
[24] *CPR 1413–16*, p. 355.
[25] *CPR 1446–52*, p. 114. The church was worth 14 marks per annum, clear value: *VCH Lincoln*, II, 159.
[26] Jacob, p. 473.
[27] Dugdale: *Baronage*, I, 130.
[28] *Monasticon*, VI, 22; K & H, p. 83. Carisbrooke was actually attached to Sheen, and worth £86 per annum.
[29] *CPR 1396–99*, p. 280.
[30] *CPR 1408–13*, p. 416.
[31] Jacob, pp. 357–8.
[32] The 1535 value was £323, which means that this was a major house: K & H, p. 134.

Three considerable foundations were begun, *de novo*, by peers between 1325 and 1350, and there was a minor house, at Flanesford, begun in 1346 (plus an abortive foundation, by Bartholomew Badlesmere). While none of the three major Austin houses ranked as a giant, in so far as the 1535 valors are an accurate guide, all were houses of comfortable means. The growth of all three reveals a continuous concern of the part of each founding family, even more than with the wealthier Charterhouses. Perhaps the popularity of the Austins lay in their ability to reconcile their own rules and the founder's desire to have a say in the affairs of the house.

Thomas Wake originally had planned to build his 'monastery of St Augustine' at Cottingham, Yorkshire, and to incorporate the church there into the foundation.[33] When this proposal proved difficult to effect, it was decided to transfer the house to nearby Haltemprice. The new priory received a royal licence, permitting it to acquire land and rent worth £20 a year. Wake gave land and rent worth £3 4s 0d towards the amount permitted in 1331.[34] After this slow start he proceeded to enrich the house steadily: the advowson of the church at Elvele, Yorkshire, land and the advowson at Belton, Lincoln, some miscellaneous pieces of Yorkshire land, the manor of Wharrum, the manor of Stowebyndon, Norfolk, 'said to be held in chief', £40 of rents from land in Cumberland, land in Deeping, the manor of Barkeston worth £9 9s 0d, scattered pieces of property worth £12 16s 0d, rents in Yorkshire and lands worth £34 11s 0d, and more lands and rents worth £7 11s 2d yearly.[35] These extensive grants all came between 1331 and 1342. During these years Wake not only satisfied the full value of the original licence to alienate, £20 per annum, but he obtained a second licence to alienate possessions worth another £20 annually, and then a third licence, this time for property worth £40.[36] His horizons broadened and his commitment deepened. The founder was appropriately buried in his own priory. The only other noble who remembered the house, designed to accommodate thirteen canons, was John Neville. In his will he left his body, along with bequests of a courser, 10 marks cash for a one-year

[33] *CPL 1305–43*, p. 210.
[34] *CPR 1330–34*, p. 67.
[35] *CPR 1330–34*, pp. 84, 151, 260; *CPR 1334–38*, pp. 277, 468, 472; *CPR 1338–40*, pp. 120, 122, 300; *CPR 1340–43*, pp. 529, 536. The monastery at Selbey, York, claimed that the advowson of Elvele was its major source of support, and they were allowed to retain it, for £40: *CPR 1348–50*, p. 504.
[36] *CPR 1338–40*, p. 97; *Ibid.*, p. 546.

chantry, and assorted vestments, and a chalice.[37] But Haltemprice really owed its existence and wealth (£100 per annum in 1535) to one man.

If Wake is associated with Haltemprice, then Montague is the name that goes with the Austin Priory at Bisham (Brustlesham), Berkshire. William Montague, earl of Salisbury, founded a canonry there, in 1337 or 1338, on the site of a former preceptory of the Temple. His first licence, obtained in 1336, permitted the alienation of the manor of Hurdcate, Somerset, and the advowson of the church at Ringwood.[38] In 1337 William was allowed to alienate this property, and to add the manor of Bisham.[39] A general licence to found and to endow was issued in October, 1337, 'with the assent of the council', and the earl was now permitted to alienate land, rent, and advowsons, 'whether held in chief or otherwise, to the value of £300'.[40]

In 1374 the Montagues were again licensed to alienate. Rents and a Lincolnshire advowson were given, 'in satisfaction of £20 7s 0d of the £300'.[41] Three years later another £40 worth of land, or rather, land declared to be in satisfaction of £40, went to the house.[42] A small grant of 1392 (land worth 7s 8d and a rental of 26s 8d) came without mention of the original licence, but was simply 'in aid of their maintenance'.[43] The priory received lands and rents (including, among others, the rent of a fourth part of a pound of cumin), reversions of land, etc., in 1392, worth £40 altogether.[44] This marked the end of the family's direct alienations. If they realized or even came close to their avowed goal of £300 the house was certainly able to fend for itself. On the other hand, the contingencies of life might eat up a more than adequate initial grant, and Bisham claimed that it suffered continual losses:[45]

Many of the houses, barns, and buildings erected by the earl have been in great measure ruined by the frequent overflowing of the Thames and by storms; that on account of divers pestilences in times past they have

[37] *TV*, p. 265.
[38] *CPR 1334–38*, p. 243.
[39] *Ibid.*, p. 552.
[40] *Ibid.*, p. 545. The formal charter of 12 Edward III is found in *Monasticon*, IV, 527.
[41] *CPR 1370–74*, p. 454.
[42] *CPR 1374–77*, pp. 463–4.
[43] *CPR 1391–96*, pp. 111–12.
[44] *CPL 1362–1404*, p. 117.
[45] *Ibid.*, p. 163.

suffered from a lack of tenants and cultivators and a murrain among their cattle, sheep and horses; that on account of the numerous guests, both rich and poor, their priory being hard by the highway and near Windsor castle, and of other causes beyond their control, their revenues are greatly reduced, and themselves heavily in debt and reduced to poverty.

So the Montagues heeded such pleas and remembered Bisham in their wills. Maud Montague received a licence to take the bones of earl John from Cirencester Abbey and to redeposit them at Bisham.[46] Earl William's daughter Philippa was buried there, and she bequeathed furniture and ornaments from her private chapel.[47] Her husband, the earl of March, left 40 marks to the house, to be used for prayers which he directed in great detail.[48] He had no objection to lying with his in-laws, rather than in one of his family's favourite sites in the west. Earl William himself left Bisham £30 for trentals and other services, 500 marks for construction and for a splendid tomb, lovingly described in his will and meant to contain him, his father, mother, and son.[49] Elizabeth Montague left money for funeral ceremonies and burial, 3,000 masses to be said as quickly as possible (£12 10s 0d sufficed for this purpose), a two-priest chantry for a year, and 400 marks for two perpetual chaplains, one canonical and one a secular, plus money for building and furnishing an altar.[50] This bequest was impressive for its volume and diversity. Matilda Montague was buried at Bisham, and she left 13s 6d to the prior, 6s 8d to each canon, and 3s 4d to the lesser clerks.[51] Thomas Montague bequeathed £100 for prayers, and he left directions about the construction of a chapel.[52] The Nevilles inherited the Montague interest in Bisham, along with their estates and titles. Richard Neville made provision in his will for burial there, and left money for a tomb and prayers.[53] He left 200 marks for the tomb, 100 marks for his funeral, two coursers, a harness of armour, his standard, and vestments from his own chapel.[54] Two of his sons also asked to be buried there.[55]

---

[46] *CPR 1416–22*, p. 312.
[47] *TV*, p. 101.
[48] *RW*, p. 110.
[49] *TV*, p. 145.
[50] Jacob, p. 15.
[51] PCC, Luffenham 2.
[52] Jacob, p. 397.
[53] *TV*, pp. 286–7.
[54] *TE*, II, 240.
[55] Dugdale: *Baronage*, I, 306, 308, and P. M. Kendall: *Warwick the Kingmaker* (London, 1947), pp. 107, 322.

The third major Austin foundation was the priory at Maxstoke, Warwick. William de Clinton had originally proposed, in 1330–1, to build a secular college or chantry chapel, and a licence in 1331 permitted him to alienate land and rent worth £20 yearly, plus the advowson of Maxstoke church. The college, of six priests, was already in existence when, in 1336, the founder decided to establish 'a monastery of canons regular of the order of St Augustine'.[56] William had been moved by 'divine inspiration', which was only sparingly released on the nobility, and the king, in order 'to further his good intentions and to be partaker of so meritorious a work, as also for the special affection' he bore William, granted the new licence.[57] These touching sentiments were translated into tangibles when the advowson of Long Itchington was added. That of Shustoke came in 1343, that of Fillongley in 1345.[58] Clinton wished to see the endowments reach £200 annual income, more than adequate support for a prior and twelve canons (nine of whom were always to be ordained).[59] Though the canonry was dedicated in 1342, new endowments continued to come from the doting father. Land and rents in Worcester and Warwick, worth in excess of £23 1s 11d, were alienated in partial satisfaction of £30, permitted under a second licence.[60] The advowson of the church at Aston Cantlow, Warwick, was granted.[61] As late as 1408 the present Lord Clinton gave the house an additional £10 in annual rents.[62]

The Clintons' concern cannot be measured solely in terms of endowments. The founder had personally gone to Rome to obtain the original papal licence for the proposed chantry,[63] and he was eventually buried in 'my priory'.[64] His interest is further borne out by the attention he paid to the regulation of various details, e.g. the clothing of the canons and their constitution. Every canon had to be[65]

Free-born or free at the time of his admission, of good and honest life, sufficiently learned for the condition of a canon regular, and possessed of a

---

[56] *CPR 1330–34*, p. 131.
[57] *CPR 1334–38*, pp. 309–10.
[58] *VCH, Warwick*, II, 91.
[59] *Ibid.*, p. 92.
[60] *CPR 1343–45*, pp. 357–8.
[61] *Ibid.*, p. 476.
[62] *VCH Warwick*, II, 92.
[63] Dugdale: *Baronage*, I, 530.
[64] *TV*, p. 55.
[65] *VCH Warwick*, II, 92.

competent voice for singing the divine service, of at least eighteen years of age, and having no impediment to entering on the priesthood when of canonical age.

William's legacy had some thorns among the flowers, and a disputed claim to the advowson at Aston Cantlow involved the house in crippling fifteenth-century litigation.[66] Maxstoke never flourished so as to rival the giant foundations, but a modest noble family did here found a house commensurate with its wealth and import.

There are two other Austin foundations to be noted. Richard Talbot received a licence in 1346 to found a house at Flanesford, Herefordshire. A full size house, with a prior and twelve or more men, may have been intended. 'But the Black Death, coming so soon after its foundations appears to have prevented it from being properly endowed or colonized, and it is doubtful if there were more than two or three canons.'[67] The other house was the abortive one which Bartholomew Badlesmere proposed to build in Kent. He was licensed to grant land and eight local advowsons,[68] but despite the confirmation of the endowment in 1330, there is no evidence that any building had ever been begun.[69] The founder was executed shortly after the granting of the original licence.

The mendicant orders did not fare too poorly. Three Franciscan houses, and one each of the Austin Friars and Franciscan Nuns were founded during this period. Founding a mendicant house, it must be remembered, was not a major financial undertaking, comparable to founding a house of canons or even a large hospital. Friaries were poor, as they were meant to be, though we may be sceptical of how much poverty they voluntarily embraced, and how much was imposed on them by necessity. A modest endowment at the time of foundation sufficed to establish a house, and the founder might never again bother with his own creation, unlike the pattern usually followed in founding the Austin canonries. A small plot of land and a bit of rental income must have gone a long way. Continuing interest was unusual, and there were few follow-up grants and bequests from the founder or other members of his family.

A licence of 1387 allowed James Butler, Earl of Ormond, to found a Franciscan house at Aylesbury, Buckinghamshire, and 'to alienate to

[66] *Ibid.*, p. 94.
[67] K & H, p. 137.
[68] *CPR 1317–21*, p. 449.
[69] *CPR 1330–34*, p. 3.

them in mortmain 10 acres of land there'.[70] Though there is no record of further benefactions from Butler, we do know that the house was meant to hold twelve friars, and therefore it must have been of moderate means.[71]

The Franciscan house at Walsingham was so well situated, near a major pilgrim shrine, that one wonders why no friary was there before 1347. Then Elizabeth de Burgh braved the opposition of the nearby Austin priory, whose patroness she was, and obtained licence to found a house of Friars Minor.[72] Clement VI allowed the provincial of the order in England to acquire a site to house a warden and twelve friars.[73] In 1348 Elizabeth bestowed 4 acres and 1 rood of land, 'whereof the 4 acres are said to be held in chief'.[74] When she died in 1355 her will left them another £5 in cash.[75] These grants, and others picked up at the time of establishment, sufficed to set up the house. Some years later the earl of March, lord of Walsingham manor, left them 40 marks, to be spent in carrying out detailed instructions about prayers.[76] Richard Scrope's gift of 6s 8d cannot have been of much further aid,[77] and at its dissolution in 1538 the house only had three remaining friars.[78] The Franciscans probably missed their mark in not establishing themselves at Walsingham a century before they did.

Knowles gives 1351 for the foundation of the Franciscan house at Ware, Hertfordshire.[79] However, Thomas Wake, lord of Lidell, had begun his labours toward that end some year earlier. In 1338 he was licensed to alienate a messuage and 7 acres there, on which the Gray Friars could build 'an oratory, houses, and other buildings'.[80] In 1344 he sought to bring four or six Dominican nuns from Brabant into England and to 'found a house of that religious body in the realm'.[81] But nothing came of this, and the Franciscans were settled, with their

[70] *CPR 1385–89*, p. 307.
[71] K & H, p. 189.
[72] *CPR 1345–48*, p. 255; K & H, p. 193. A large hospice for the accommodation of poor pilgrims was attached to the house. This would hardly have helped the friary in its desire to allay the jealousy of its neighbours.
[73] *VCH Norfolk*, II, 436.
[74] *CPR 1348–50*, p. 7.
[75] *RW*, p. 33.
[76] *Ibid.*, p. 110.
[77] *TE*, III, 298.
[78] K & H, p. 193.
[79] K & H, p. 194.
[80] *CPR 1338–40*, p. 14.
[81] *CPR 1343–45*, p. 339.

possessions confirmed by the Pope, in 1350–1.[82] There is no further record of endowments from the founder, but his original grant seemingly sufficed. While the friary at Ware was never particularly popular, it got £10 in 1381 from William Latimer, and 6s 8d in Richard Scrope of Bolton's will.[83]

The foundations of the house of Austin Friars at Atherstone, Warwick, in 1375 by Ralph Basset of Drayton was a unique benefaction to this order.[84] The foundation licence only assigned 12 acres of land in the town.[85] But Basset's will provided a gift of 500 marks towards completion of the church and buildings. It seems the sum was never forthcoming, for the 1535 valor indicated a total annual income of but £2 18s 0d, and only 30s 2d as clear income.[86]

The most interesting act of foundation was that for the house of Franciscan nuns at Denney, Cambridge. Marie de St Pol, widow of the earl of Pembroke, was what the church dreamed of by way of a patroness; widowed while quite young, rich, pious, with no children and no close relatives in England. In 1333 she had been granted an indult to enter monasteries of religious women, with a retinue of six matrons.[87] While this was as close as she ever came to taking the veil herself, in 1336 she turned her attention toward making a *de novo* foundation.[88] She alienated the manor of Denney to the Franciscan nuns of Waterbeach, as a contribution 'towards their sustenance and to found and maintain certain chantries and alms'.[89] The king gave her the licence in return for 'her good services', mostly for diplomatic work on the continent, where she had friends and influence. But the widow soon changed her mind about endowing Waterbeach, and in 1341 she received a licence to erect a new house at Denney.[90]

By 1346 Marie had decided that the old house at Waterbeach was to be closed, its nuns moved to Denney, and its revenues used for the

---

[82] *CPL 1342–62*, p. 394.

[83] *TE*, I, 114; *TE*, III, 298.

[84] A. Gwynn: *The English Austin Friars in the Time of Wyclif* (Oxford, 1940), p. 16.

[85] *CPR 1374–77*, p. 183.

[86] *VCH Warwick*, II, 106; W. Dugdale: *Antiquities of Warwickshire* (London, 1730 edition), p. 108.

[87] *CPL 1305–42*, p. 393.

[88] She may have been a Franciscan tertiary at this time; Hilary Jenkinson: 'Mary de Sancto Paulo, Foundress of Pembroke College, Cambridge', *Archaeologia*, LXVI (1915), p. 420.

[89] *CPR 1334–38*, p. 248.

[90] *CPR 1340–43*, p. 289.

new house.[91] The houses were to be united in personnel and legal existence. The Waterbeach nuns were divided about this high-handed treatment, and it was not until 1351, after the rebels had been crushed, that the older house was finally and completely abandoned. In 1349, after the abbess and greater part of the sisters had left, those remaining behind banded together to elect an abbess and to receive more novices. Disputes arose between the houses, and it took several years for the Countess to enlist adequate papal and episcopal aid on behalf of Denney.[92] It is hard to see what lesson should be drawn— that the autocratic interests of a founder could be intensely unpopular among the religious? Or that the usually smooth *modus vivendi* between benefactor and ecclesiastical system could easily be disrupted by a few troublemakers. The odds in the fight always were in favour of the countess.

But at least Marie was not an ungenerous autocrat. The 1535 income of the house was £172. She alienated the manor of Strode to the house, 'cum pertinentiis quod de nobis tenetur in capite, ut dicitur simul cum litertatibus, liberis consuetudinibus, ac aliis ad idem manerium spectantibus'.[93] Then came the advowson of the church at Godreston, Suffolk, and then the advowson of Grantesdon, which Marie had granted to St Paul's but now realienated, 'for the support of divine works as she shall appoint'.[94] A few years later the Countess assigned land in Chesterton, with which she had been enfeoffed by the abbot of St Andrew, Vercelli.[95] More property followed over the years: the manor of Eyehall, Cambridge, land in Horningsey, the advowson of Eltesle.[96] General protection was procured for the nuns, their men and servants, land, rents, and possessions.[97] Marie had other religious interests, e.g. an abortive Carthusian foundation at Horne[98] and Pembroke Hall at Cambridge. But through all her activities she remembered her nuns, asking to be buried there in the habit of a sister of the order. In her will she left £100 to the abbess and sisters, 'en aide de lur besoignes', as well as 5 marks to the abbess, 10s per sister, and a half mark per friar, plus the miscellaneous relics and

[91] *CPR 1345–48*, p. 119; *Monasticon*, VI, 1550.

[92] *CPL 1342–62*, pp. 285–6.

[93] *Monasticon*, VI, 1550; *CPR 1340–43*, p. 529.

[94] *CPR 1343–45*, pp. 340, 3.

[95] *CPR 1345–48*, p. 369.

[96] *CPR 1364–67*, p. 48; *CPR 1367–70*, p. 246; *CPR 1364–67*, p. 221.

[97] *CPR 1348–50*, p. 545.

[98] *CPR 1342–62*, p. 226; she sought to endow this house with lands and rents worth £10 per annum.

chapel furnishings she had given over the years.[99] This was rather grand benefaction, almost solely the work of one woman.

Hospitals were another popular institution. Their historian lists some 750 different ones, with another fifty being uncertain.[100] By the end of the thirteenth century the bulk of them had been founded, and there were almost as many dissolutions as new foundations in the fourteenth and fifteenth centuries. While the nobles did not neglect the hospitals, the number of new foundations is rather small. Their neglect, to judge them harshly, must be judged in light of the amount of endowment needed to found a hospital. They ranged greatly in size, in the number of clerics employed, and in the number of supported indigents. But despite this diversity, the nobles could only claim credit for having founded ten hospitals, and there is doubt about some of these. Five of the ten were from the fifteenth century, two from the 1390s, one from the 1380s, one from the 1370s, and the earliest from 1342. So what activity there was took place long after the great age of foundation. If we consider the fifteenth century the prime era of 'private' religious foundations, we can see how the hospitals were fitted, by their founders, into this category. They too were considered as super-chantries, and their medical or hostelling role was of secondary importance.

Ralph Neville built a house at Welle, Yorkshire, for a master, two priests, and twenty-four brothers and sisters. He enriched his endowment with twelve messuages, twelve cottages, 300 acres of land and thirty of meadow, and the advowson of the church at Welle.[101] In 1365 he alienated more land, after paying £15 for the licence from the chancery.[102] This second benefaction was for divine services, 'according to the tenor of a special ordinance' already made.[103] John Neville left an advowson worth £40; if that were not instituted, 80 marks in land, so that 2d or 3d could be paid daily to the inmates, and 10 marks annually to the master.[104] In 1470 Lady Jane Neville bequeathed two gowns.[105] The value of the house in 1535 was placed at £42 12s 3d, with a clear income of £20 17s 11d.[106]

[99] Jenkinson: *op. cit.*, pp. 432–3.
[100] R. M. Clay: *The Medieval Hospital*, p. xviii.
[101] *CPR 1340–43*, p. 427.
[102] *CPR 1364–67*, p. 60.
[103] Dugdale: *Baronage*, I, 295.
[104] *Wills and Inventories*, II, 41.
[105] *North Country Wills*, p. 56.
[106] *Monasticon*, VI, 702.

The 'maisondieu' at Hull which Michael de la Pole founded in 1376 was an independent institution only until 1394, when it was refounded in connection with the Charterhouse there. The family had planned for some years to build the hospital, and Michael's father had obtained a licence to endow as far back as 1354, when he planned to bring the annual income up to the splendid figure of 200 marks.[107] Richard Scrope threw in the advowson of Medburn. In 1365 de la Pole paid £10 to convert his unbuilt hospital into a house of Franciscan nuns, with an abbess, twelve nuns, and a 'certain number' of poor persons.[108] This licence was vacated when the founder decided, in 1377, to build the Charterhouse, 'as it is believed that God will be served with more vigilance and devotion there by them than by women'.[109] The hospital, for thirteen poor men and thirteen poor women, went along with this. William left another £20 in his will, in 1365.[110] In 1408 the earl of Suffolk made a further grant, in conjunction with Edmund de la Pole, 'chivaler', and a clerk, Robert Bolton: four tofts, two gardens, three bovates, and thirty-three acres of arable, ten of meadow, six of pasture, and £9 8s 2d in rent, in aid of the maintenance.[111] The large endowment originally envisaged got lost amid all the activity, for the 1535 valor showed a gross income of only about £32 19s 9d.[112]

The earl of Arundel founded the hospital of Holy Trinity at Arundel in 1380, the year he obtained licence to establish a secular college there. The hospital was for twenty poor, 'valetudinary or aged, and (who) had been attached to the manors of his father, and unmarried or widowers, and who were not allowed to marry after their admission, upon pain of removal'.[113] As well as a grant of four messuages and two tofts,[114] the house profited under Earl Thomas's will in 1415, and the income stood at £101 13s 10¼d in 1437, at £94 in 1546.[115]

The hospital at Brackley, Northampton, was an ancient foundation, fallen into ruin and without inmates, when the Lovels became con-

---

[107] *CPR 1354–58*, p. 158.
[108] *CPR 1364–67*, p. 153.
[109] *CPR 1374–77*, pp. 470–1.
[110] *TE*, I, 76.
[111] *CPR 1408–13*, p. 57.
[112] *Monasticon*, VI, 736.
[113] *Ibid.*
[114] *CPR 1391–96*, p. 562.
[115] *VCH Sussex*, II, 98.

cerned with it.[116] At first Maud Lovel wanted to convert it into a Dominican house for ten men.[117] Endowments were planned, but the Dominican house never materialized. By 1425 Francis Lovel had re-established the hospital, and in its short life—it was annexed to Magdalen College in 1484 for 400 marks—both property and attention were lavished on the hospital. It was for travellers, not residents—an unusual feature—and there were four or six beds for 'the free relief of poor travellers for one night or longer if necessary'.[118] Each week six loaves, at 3d each, were distributed to the poor. The house's statutes reflect the Lovel's concern.[119] They insisted the clerics be adequately educated: 'beside the master (there is to be) two suitable chaplains, who may have the understanding of reading and singing, competently skilled in letters and approved in life, manners, behaviour, and apparel.'[120] Instructions were given about prayers, services and vestments, and the inalienability of the endowment was emphasized.

The hospital at Ewelme, Oxford, was founded in 1437, when a licence to William and Alice de la Pole empowered them to establish an alms-house and to endow it with land to the value of 100 marks. They paid 250 marks for this licence, and they completed their endowments in 1442 by granting the manors of Conock, Rambridge, and Marsh Gibbon, along with the advowson of the latter church, altogether worth £59.[121] The hospital was for two chaplains and thirteen indigents, and it included a free school. Each inmate received 14d per week, a generous sum by the standards of the day.[122] The elaborate statutes of the house have been printed,[123] and it suffices here to note the concern that the masters and teachers be properly trained and diligent in their duties. The prayers, through the hours of the day and the times of the year, were elaborated by the founders. Life may have been secure, but it was heavily regulated. The de la Poles made no further endowments, though Lady Alice's magnificent

[116] For its earlier history, see *Baronage*, I, 559.

[117] G. Baker: *History of Northamptonshire* (Northampton, 1822), I, 581.

[118] *VCH Northampton*, II, 153.

[119] No mention of the hospital appears in the will of William, Lord Lovel, in 1455: *Lincoln Diocese Documents* (ed., Andrew Clark), Early English Text Society, o.s., CXLIX (1914), pp. 70–87.

[120] For the Brackley statutes, *Visitation of Religious Houses in the Diocese of Lincoln* (ed., A. H. Thompson), Canterbury and York Society, pp. 15–21.

[121] *CPR 1436–41*, p. 80; *CPR 1441–46*, p. 60.

[122] Dugdale: *Baronage*, II, 187.

[123] *Historical Manuscript Commission*, IX, 217–22.

tomb and chantry must have brought a considerable sum to the house. The 1526 income was listed at £64, almost exactly the amount of the original endowment.[124]

The Hungerfords began the hospital at Heytesbury, Wiltshire in 1449, though it was only complete in 1472, when Margaret Hungerford alienated the manors of Cheverell, Burnell, and Cheverell Magna. The hospital, meant for a priest-warden, twelve poor men, and a female servant, was granted power to plead and to be impleaded.[125] Lady Hungerford gave the right of appointing the *custos* of the hospital to the chancellor of Salisbury, and the right of visiting and of examining the statutes to the chapter there, and of nominating tenants to the lord of the manor of Heytesbury, 'with this restriction only, that he should give the preference to old and meritorious servants of the house of Hungerford'.[126] It sounds as though she was willing to honour her husband's wishes but had no further interest in the hospital once it became a going concern.[127]

The hospital of St Leonard at Alkmonton, Derby, was substantially built, if not actually founded, by Walter Blount, Lord Mountjoy.[128] He left lands which returned £10 per annum, in return for prayers for himself, his children, his ancestors, the Duke of Buckingham, the Earl Rivers, etc. The seven inmates, old servants of the Lordship of Barton (held by Blount) or other tenants of his in Derby and Stafford-shire, were to repeat St Mary's psalter twice daily. These men, all fifty-five years old and more, were to get room, board, 2s 4d per week, and a gown of white or russet clothe every three years. Begging would lead to their dismissal. The master was to say a yearly mass on St Nicholas's day. The other obligation incumbent upon him was to wear a gown of any colour but red or green, with a blue *tau* cross on the left side. But since the hospital 'appears to have enjoyed the happiness of having no history', we know little more about the patron's endow-ment or concern.[129]

Two other hospitals can be briefly mentioned. That at Donnington,

[124] K & H, p. 277.
[125] *Monasticon*, VI, 724.
[126] *Ibid.*, VI, 725; R. Hoare: *Modern Wiltshire*, I, 125.
[127] Though Margaret did stipulate that the keeper of the hospital could hold no other living: M. A. Seymour: 'The Organisation, Personnel, and Function of the Medieval Hospital in the Later Middle Ages', London M.A., 1946, p. 122; A. F. Leach: *The Schools of Medieval England* (New York, 1915), pp. 272–3.
[128] S. Glover: *History and Gazetteer of Derbyshire* (Derby, 1833), II, part 1, p. 16. K & H, p. 251, for a foundation date of 1100.
[129] *VCH Derby*, II, 81.

Berkshire, founded in 1393, is attributed to Richard Abberbury.[130] But Dugdale speaks of Michael de la Pole as the founder, and says that he endowed it to the tune of 14d per week per inmate, of which there were 13.[131] This comes to about £40 per annum, a sizeable sum. The hospital at Bridgwater, Somerset, dedicated to St John, had originally been founded in 1213. But in 1457 William, Lord Zouche, and the Duke of York were referred to as 'founders and patrons'.[132] These terms were loosely applied to many benefactors in the middle ages and they need not be taken literally. But they do offer evidence of considerable support of the establishment.

In summary we can say that those nobles who did found hospitals were tolerably generous. If few could emulate the style of benefaction practised by the founders of Ewelme or Arundel, most establishments were for a dozen or more indigents, as well as for clerks, servants, and assorted extras. Only Brackley was primarily meant to serve travellers, rather than permanent residents. Other hospitals were for the aged, more than for the ill, and for the repayment of old family servants. Where the statutes are available they show the founders to have been concerned, almost to the point of petty interference and dictatorial regulation. The nobles wanted thanks while they were alive, prayers for their souls after death, and the right to control and regulate their beneficiaries at both times.

Large numbers of secular colleges were founded in late medieval England, being mostly colleges of chantry priests. Some of the colleges shown in Table 6, e.g. Elmley, North Cadbury, and Ruthin do not properly qualify for treatment here. Others are clear-cut examples of foundations, de novo, by the nobles. Thomas Astley founded a large chantry and then converted it into a college at Astley, Warwick. He had originally alienated 'eight messuages, two carucates of land, pasture for two horses and four oxen, and 106s 8d in rent', for the priests.[133] Then he added the advowson of the church at Astley. In 1340 more land was alienated, 'toward the sustenance' of the seven men now praying at Astley.[134] By now Lord Thomas sought to make them an independent corporate body, and he peti-

---

[130] Clay: op. cit., p. 279.
[131] Dugdale: Baronage, II, 189.
[132] Monasticon, VI, 662; CPR 1422–29, p. 23; VCH Somerset, II, 156.
[133] CPR 1334–38, p. 389; Dugdale: Antiquities of Warwickshire, pp. 109–10, for the founder's endowments.
[134] CPR 1338–40, pp. 162, 526.

tioned to do so, 'for the honour of God and the glory of the Church'.[135] Shortly afterwards the proud father alienated the advowson of Hillmorton church to the college, and the advowson of the church at Long Stanton was given three years later by the Earl of Warwick.[136] In 1361 the founder increased the endowment by another £9 15s 0½d, adding rentals in Warwick and Nottingham, and his son added £2 annual rent in 1389.[137] The college held a dean, two canons, three vicars, plus clerks and servants, and their lives were minutely regulated by ordinances governing both financial and spiritual activities. When instituted, clerks had 'to take an oath to observe the statutes and ordinances of the college, and to abstain from revealing in the least degree the secrets of the chapter'.[138] Though a beautiful church was built, the institution was never a large one, and its 1535 income of £39 certainly indicated a modest size.

John Cobham founded a college of five priests, one of whom was to be the master, in 1362 in the church at Cobham, Kent. He paid £30 for the royal licence to alienate pieces of land and a rent of 21 quarters and 3 bushels of barley.[139] It was not until 1367 that Cobham's foundation was licensed to acquire land and rents to the value of £40 per annum.[140] As was so often the case with new foundations, a series of smallish endowments were made within a short span; a messuage and 80 acres and 5 marks rent in 1369; a messuage, a mill, 160 acres of arable, 200 of pasture, 15 of wood, again in 1369.[141] The bishop of Rochester gave an advowson, after the exchange of some property with Cobham, since it seems that the college was already 'impoverished by pestilences and other misfortunes which for some time prevailed more than is wont in the parts of England'.[142]

Gradually the endowment was built up, and the net income was £128 in 1535. A papal letter of 1405 states that the income was not to exceed 200 marks, nor that of the two advowsons being appropriated, 30 marks.[143] By 1389 the original five chaplains had become nine, and their number had grown to eleven in 1390.[144]

[135] CPR 1343–45, pp. 1–2.
[136] CPR 1343–45, p. 114; CPR 1345–48, p. 131.
[137] VCH Warwick, II, p. 119.
[138] Ibid., p. 118.
[139] CPR 1361–64, p. 265.
[140] CPR 1367–70, p. 387.
[141] CPR 1367–70, pp. 250, 282.
[142] CPL 1362–1404, p. 226.
[143] CPL 1404–15, pp. 28–9.
[144] VCH Kent, II, 231.

Cobham sought to exalt his college, also his burial site,[145] by procuring indulgences for visitors. He obtained a relaxation, 'during 10 years, of 100 days of enjoined penance to penitents who on the principle feasts of the year visit the college'.[146] This was renewed in 1391, for a relaxation of five years for those who 'visit and give alms for the conservation of the Church'.[147] And in 1405 the indulgence was to cover visitors coming on the Feast of St Mary Magdalen, 'from the first to the second vespers'.[148] This method of popularizing a college, and of adding to its revenues, was rarely practised, though its wisdom seems obvious to us.[149]

The Greystokes were the only family among the nobility with their base in Cumberland. In 1358 William Greystoke proposed to convert the rectory of Greystoke into a secular college. He paid 80 marks for a licence to alienate land and the advowson there.[150] But his death in 1359 put a halt to the scheme, and not until 1374 did his son receive a renewal of the licence. Now the project was seriously begun. The value of the church and property was said to be, in 1379, £100, and though there were three chaplains and three clerks attached, the episcopal commissioners held that 'it would be to the greater glory of God if the number of ministering clergy were increased'.[151] Papal licence to build a college of seven perpetual chaplains came in 1381. John Greystoke bequeathed the house a horse, as a mortuary payment, plus arms, vestments, chapel ornaments, and lead with which to repair the choir.[152] The college embraced the local church. In 1535 its yearly income stood at £82, of which £42 6s 8d went for pensions, and each chantry priest received £3 6s 8d per annum for victuals and a like sum for his private use.[153]

The FitzAlan college at Arundel was a much grander affair. On the site of an old Benedictine cell a collegiate church was proposed in 1354, though not actually built until 1380. The earl was licensed in 1375 to alienate a yearly rent of 107 marks, from his Sussex manors, to support the chaplains of the chantry until 'they be provided

[145] He left £5 as a cash bequest in his will: *TV*, p. 69.
[146] *CPL 1362–1404*, p. 62.
[147] *Ibid.*, p. 396.
[148] *CPL 1404–15*, p. 27.
[149] For other examples, furnished respectively by the Beauchamps and the Bassets, see: *CPL 1362–1404*, p. 39, 38.
[150] *CPR 1358–61*, p. 46.
[151] *VCH Cumberland*, II, 206.
[152] *TE*, I, 85.
[153] *VCH Cumberland*, II, 207.

with an equivalent in land or rent'.[154] With death approaching, he left 1,000 marks in his will, enabling the house to purchase land. It was to support six priests and three choristers, and the earl believed, probably correctly, that the income from his bequest would suffice.[155] The foundation licence of 1380 authorized the suppression of St Nicholas's priory, a cell subject to the alien priory of Séez. The Earl paid £40 for this licence, and during the war with France the master and chaplains were to pay £20 yearly for the windfall.[156] More alienations were to come: the advowson of Goring church, plus 202 marks in rent, converted in 1386 to alienated land of equivalent value.[157]

The college was of good size, having a master, vice-master, precentor, ten chaplains, two deacons and two sub-deacons, and four choristers.[158] Earl Thomas left £133 6s 8d for funeral masses, plus sums for the building of his tomb.[159] Countess Joan, when buried there, left £40 for her soul, and two gowns.[160] Countess Eleanor was likewise interred there, and she bequeathed £40 also for annual prayers. Her executors were authorized to spend 200 marks to build a perpetual chantry in her honour at the altar of Our Lady, with a priest specially employed for at least twenty years, at 10 marks per annum.[161] So for almost a century we see that the FitzAlans continued to spend lavishly for the college wherein many of them chose to await the second coming.

The Nevilles built two fifteenth-century colleges, that at Staindrop and that of St William in York. The Durham college was more of a hospital, for 'it seems probable that the Earl intended the house to serve as a place of retirement for his retainers and servants when they grew old or infirm'.[162] The licence of foundation allowed the alienation of 2 messuages and 12 acres of arable in Staindrop, plus the advowson of the church.[163] The advowson of Latham parish church was added in 1409.[164] The college housed a master, six priests, six

[154] *CPR 1374–77*, p. 129.
[155] *TV*, p. 95.
[156] *CPR 1377–81*, p. 494; *VCH Suffolk*, II, 108.
[157] *CPR 1381–85*, pp. 38, 66; *Monasticon,* VI, 1379; *VCH Suffolk* II, 109; *CPR 1385–89*, p. 78.
[158] *RW*, pp. 122–3.
[159] Jacob, p. 74.
[160] *Ibid.*, p. 541.
[161] *TV*, p. 277.
[162] *VCH Durham*, II, 129.
[163] *CPR 1408–13*, p. 35.
[164] *Ibid.*, p. 145.

clerks, six esquires, six grooms, and six poor people.[165] The founder again chose to be buried there, and in his will left more bequests: two horses, 300 marks to complete the construction, all the vestments of his own chapel, £1 per chaplain, and 6s 8d for each other man in the hospital.[166]

The large and wealthy college at Stoke-by-Clare was a foundation of Edmund Mortimer, but he did little to set up the house. A wealthy alien priory dependent upon Bec, the house had been naturalized in 1395.[167] Edmund petitioned in 1415 that it be changed to a college of seculars. It maintained a dean and six canons, eight vicars, two upper and two under clerks, five choristers, a teaching master, and a variety of minor officials and servants.[168] The endowments did not come from Mortimer coffers, but from the possessions of the old cell. The founder largely contented himself with using his influence to gain the licence of foundation and to see that the old revenues were not disbursed.

Thomas de la Warre was the rector of Manchester church. In 1427 he received permission to build a collegiate church, and he endowed it with £200 in land.[169] The founder was summoned to parliament as a peer when his brother, 4th baron de la Warre died, and he took his new project seriously; he paid 200 marks for the royal licence. Thomas, as a former priest, may have had a strong religious leaning. He was also without a direct heir, and he may have wanted a spiritual memorial before the family estates passed to his nephew, Reynold West. The house was worth £213 in the 1535 assessment, almost exactly the original value.

Lord Cromwell founded a college at Tattershall, with an attached almshouse, to go with his great new castle there. The Cromwells had long been local patrons there,[170] but in 1439 they began in earnest, with a licence permitting them to[171]

---

[165] Dugdale: *Baronage*, I, 298; R. Surtees: *History of Durham* (London, 1840), IV, 134.

[166] *Wills and Inventories*, p. 69.

[167] D. Mathew: *The Norman Monasteries and their English Possessions* (Oxford, 1962), pp. 44, 111.

[168] *VCH Suffolk*, II, 145; J. H. Wylie: *The Reign of Henry V* (Cambridge, 1914), I, 350–4, for a summary of the statutes.

[169] F. R. Raines (ed.): *The Rectors of Manchester and the Wardens of the Collegiate Church*, Chetham Society, V (1885).

[170] *CPL 1362–1404*, p. 350; *CPR 1388–92*, p. 3.

[171] *CPR 1436–41*, p. 292.

transform the church at Tateshale into a collegiate church of 7 chaplains, 6 secular clerks, and 7 choristers, 1 of the chaplains to be master or warden, and to erect a perpetual almshouse for 13 poor persons of either sex ... License also for the master or warden and chaplains of the college to appropriate the said church and to purchase additional lands, tenements, rents and advowsons to the additional value of £200.

A licence of 1453 permitted the alienation of property worth £150 13s 4d towards the full value, and the next year another £32 in land and rents was alienated.[172] The founder was buried there, with bequests of £40 and his chapel ornaments.[173]

The Nevilles befriended York Minster by establishing a college dedicated to St William, to house 'the chantry priests of the cathedral, one of whom is to be provost'. The founders were George Neville, bishop of Exeter, and the Earl of Warwick. However, they exercised a light hand in making endowments. The licence to found carried no mention of gifts. Rather, it authorized the dean and chapter, not the lay founders, to grant lands and tenements. The college was empowered to acquire 'lands to the value of £100 yearly',[174] but its income in 1535 was only £22.

Several other establishments deserve passing mention. Guy Beauchamp sought to build a college at Elmley in 1309. But the endowment was inadequate, and it was reduced to a chantry.[175] The earl wanted eight chaplains to live on a gift of £20 in land, to come from the manor of Wickwane and the advowson of Elmley church.[176] The Beauchamps did continue to favour the establishment, and when Earl Thomas bequeathed it, in 1400, some vestments, he referred to it as 'my college'.[177] North Cadbury college had an uncertain status, and it may never have been incorporated as a college. Elizabeth Botreaux was licensed by Henry V to found and to endow a college, for seven secular chaplains, one of whom was to be rector, and for four clerks, together capable of acquiring property worth 100 marks yearly, plus additional land for a manse.[178] Ralph Basset's chantry

[172] *CPR 1452–61*, pp. 161, 195.
[173] *TE*, II, 197. Also, Leach: *op. cit.*, p. 256, for the provisions supporting a grammar master.
[174] *CPR 1461–67*, p. 74; F. Harrison: *op. cit.*, pp. 309, 313.
[175] K & H, p. 329; T. Nash: *Collection for a History of Worcester* (1781), I, 382, 390–2, for the foundation charters.
[176] *CPR 1307–13*, p. 136; *VCH Worcester*, III, 346.
[177] *TV*, p. 154.
[178] *Monasticon*, VI, 1423; *CPR 1422–29*, p. 190.

at Sapcote may have aspired to collegiate status.[179] He was licensed to alienate £10 yearly, land and rent, to two chaplains,[180] but he never made the big commitment that usually accompanied the transformation of a church into a full college. Scrope of Bolton requested a licence to make the parish church at Wensley, Yorkshire, into a college, but there is no evidence that he ever alienated much of the £150 worth of property which a royal licence had permitted.[181]

Lord John Willoughby's connections with Spilsby college are tenuous. His death, after papal and royal licence to create the college, had been gained, ended his plans to endow a master and twelve chaplains. Though the college was built, there is no further record of the Willoughby concern after the original licence of 1347.[182] Reginald Cobham was a leading figure among the founders of Lingfield college in Surrey. It was granted 3 messuages and 38 acres of land, all that Cobham was licensed to alienate.[183] Nothing at all came of William Kerdeston's proposal to build a college for thirteen chaplains at Claxton, Norfolk,[184] and it is likely that many other nobles made plans which never came to fruition. Between the intention and the creation lay dreams, petitions, and endowments, all apt to put off the well-intentioned but irresolute.

The academic foundations of the nobles hardly detain us. Buckingham college at Cambridge was a minor hostel there, for the use of Benedictines. Its major benefactor seems to have been Humphrey Stafford.[185] Clare Hall and Pembroke Hall, Cambridge, were both major and lasting foundations. Each was the child of a great dowager patroness. Elizabeth de Burgh and Marie de St Pol, already founders of mendicant houses, were good friends and probably influenced each other. They, like all the other nobles, ignored Oxford completely.

In 1326 the king licensed the creation of a college at Cambridge known as University Hall. It made its uncertain way for a few years, but fire destroyed it and left it without prospects. In 1336 Elizabeth first indicated her concern, and she was licensed to assign the advowson of Litlington church to 'the master and scholars of the hall of the

---

[179] K & H, p. 355.
[180] *CPR 1370–74*, p. 232.
[181] *CPR 1396–99*, p. 489.
[182] *VCH Lincoln*, II, 236; K & H, p. 342.
[183] Manning: *History of Surrey*, II, 352–3; *VCH Surrey*, II, 127–8.
[184] *CPL 1342–62*, p. 142.
[185] *Lincoln Visitations*, II, 55.

university of Cambridge'.[186] The founder, Richard de Badew, surrendered his rights in 1338, and sometime afterwards the name was changed to Clare Hall.[187] Elizabeth continued to endow the college: the advowsons of the churches at Grantesdon and at Dokesworth were turned over to the academic foundation. These churches were worth 50 and 25 marks respectively, so she was not simply making an empty gesture.[188] The hall was soon brought to its intended complement of a master and fifteen scholars,[189] and in her will the patroness left another £40, plus books and ornaments.[190]

When Marie de St Pol founded Pembroke Hall in 1347 there were only four endowed colleges at Cambridge. The king's licence allowed her to 'found a house of scholars in Cambridge and to establish there a warden and 30 scholars or more at her will, living under a certain rule and studying in divers faculties'. They could acquire property to the value of £100 yearly.[191] Lands in Derby and Rutland, originally assigned to Westminster Abbey, were now redirected to Cambridge.[192] The chapel was the first exclusively collegiate chapel in Cambridge. From the solid foundation that Marie laid the college established itself, and its 1535 income was £153.[193] This compares well with that of other pre-Tudor colleges, with the exception of the giant royal foundation, King's College.

[186] *CPR 1334–38*, p. 237.
[187] J. R. Wardale: *Clare College* (London, 1899), p. 3.
[188] *CPR 1345–48*, pp. 135–6; *CPL 1342–62*, p. 253.
[189] Wardale: *op. cit.*, p. 4; *CPL 1342–62*, p. 269.
[190] *RW*, p. 39; *VCH Cambridge*, III, 345; *CPR 1350–54*, p. 510.
[191] *CPR 1345–48*, p. 444.
[192] *CPR 1348–50*, p. 349.
[193] A. Attwater: *Pembroke College* (Cambridge, 1936), p. 8; *CPL 1362–1404*, p. 58.

5

<hr style="border: 1px dotted;" />

Endowments to burial churches

<hr style="border: 1px dotted;" />

In this and the next chapter we concentrate on the analysis of materials found in the wills of the nobles. If it is of some substance a will contains a large number of separate, disconnected bequests. Furthermore, such a will usually embodies a number of different kinds of bequests; no matter what we are searching for, it is intrinsically hard to see how bequests to relatives, friends, servants, confessors, poor people at one's funeral, monasteries, cathedral churches, political allies, mendicant houses, the tenants on one's manors, parish churches, hospitals, etc., can be lumped together, especially when the bequests take the forms of cash, vestments, jewels, household possessions, relics, books, furniture, and other oddments. Accordingly, in these last two chapters we can only select a few particular aspects of the testamentary bequests.

In making a will one was primarily concerned with subsidizing prayer services, as we have seen. One was also interested in disposing of one's personal possessions and in honouring, rewarding, and remembering one's friends (both personal and institutional). All these activities, taken in aggregate, can be seen as representing an effort to shape the world one could control, not only for the last time but in some ways perhaps for the first time. A man of great wealth and large family is never as free of external obligations as when he makes his last will and testament. So in these chapters we are not just following the transfer of the possessions of the aristocracy. We are assessing their sense of priorities, the way in which they arranged themselves into their world view, at the moment when they had maximum control and maximum freedom. As such, we learn about family structures, the appeal of branches of the church and parts of the realm, the

ties between husband and wife, and the competition and rivalry between the different peers, as well as about the exchange of goods. But
this is not surprising, for we said in our introduction that gift-giving
was a moral and social activity, as well as an economic one.

This chapter treats the bequests left to the ecclesiastical institutions
which served as burial houses. Most wills, even the tersest, usually
specify the place of desired burial, and most nobles were willing to
subsidize a funeral ending in an interment. They made a solemn,
deathbed commitment towards a particular place. We would expect
that they harboured some special affection for these establishments in
which they chose to lie through all eternity. In keeping with our
materialistic orientation, we seek to gauge and to assess their affec-
tions by means of a study of their subsidies.

We have already considered what the patterns of prayer endowment tell us about the concept and definition of the family. A survey
of the manner and site of burial are also of interest in an evaluation of
the reality of these bonds, which can best be studied through these
and other such behavioural definitions. New departures from family
traditions of burial and burial bequests are not always explicable, but
they do furnish information in regard to how tradition-oriented the
nobles were. How often did they act in an individualistic fashion?
And what can we learn by analysing the amount of endowment going
to the burial church, as well as the form the endowments took—cash,
personal possessions, property?

Table 7 analyses the burial site for 195 nobles, with an attempt to
calculate the type of ecclesiastical foundations chosen for the burial
house.

The 195 wills actually enable us to plot the burial sites of about 240
people, for it was common practice for a testator to state that he was

TABLE 7 Percentage of burial sites specified in wills

Type of house	Fourteenth century	Fifteenth century	Total %	Total numbers
Regular	48	39	43	83
Secular	26	39	34	66
Mendicant	18	14	15	30
Cathedral	8	8	8	16
Total	100	100	100	195

to be laid to rest in a known church, near a wife, parent, or other relative already there. Cadet branches of a family might choose to be buried near more famous kinsmen. But these other relatives have not been tallied for Table 7: only those making their own wills have been taken into account.

Though our main concern here is in the endowments which accompanied burial, it is of interest to consider the type of sites chosen. The percentage of fourteenth century wills with an expressed desire for burial in a regular house is only slightly higher than the fifteenth-century figure: 48 per cent of the fourteenth-century wills, as against 39 per cent of the fifteenth century ones. This was not a great drop for the regulars, despite what we are often told (and have seen above) about their declining popularity, a phenomenon not often questioned. In absolute terms the mendicant houses retained their popularity also —fifteen burials in each century—but the percentage of peers being buried in such houses declined from 18 per cent in the fourteenth century to 14 per cent. Various secular branches of the church gained in the fifteenth century. They attracted twice as many burials, in absolute numbers (44 as against 22: 39 per cent of the burials in the fifteenth century, compared with 26 per cent in the fourteenth). This was a definite but certainly a limited gain in popularity for the secular branches of the church.

The popularity of the regular houses is rather unexpected: 43 per cent of the nobles tallied chose them. Perhaps their decline, seen in other data, reflects a reluctance of people *in media vitae* to endow them. But on the deathbed older and more conservative traditions asserted themselves, and the nobles now thought of institutions which represented an older ethos of popular religion. No other aspect of popular religion or of philanthropy has shown the regular orders benefiting from 40 per cent of the relevant fifteenth century activity. In the span of the two centuries, more nobles (in absolute terms) were buried in monasteries and nunneries than in any other type of ecclesiastical institution. And if they were all generally popular, the Benedictine houses fared particularly well. Thirteen different houses of Black Monks held the mortal remains of 26 nobles, 9 from the fourteenth century and 17 from the fifteenth. Though Tewkesbury, Abbotsbury, St Agatha at Richmond, and the Cluniac house at Lewes each held several peers, such old houses as that at Glastonbury, Bury St Edmunds, and Battle also come in for mention.

There was the usual predilection for the Austin Canons. Fifteen of their houses were chosen as burial sites, as against thirteen Benedictine houses, but only twenty-five people were buried in the Austin houses. Guisborough hosted three burials, and Bisham six. Christ Church, London, and Stone, among others, drew no other forms of endowment from the nobles except those accompanying a burial. It is strange that men would lie forever in a house, and choose to enrich it at the time of their death, when through their active years they never alienated a plot of land or a few shillings' rent.

The houses of other orders were chosen less often. The great days of Cistercian growth and benefaction had ended, but old traditions lingered. Seven Cistercian houses received ten bodies. Jervaulx and Rievaulx had two peers each. The Carthusians only drew three people whose wills we have—John Mowbray and two de la Poles—and all were interred in houses they founded. This highlights the way in which the statistically impressive popularity of the order hung on a mere handful of patrons, for no one else was attracted to burial in a Charterhouse out of the whole range of some 85 noble families. Two people asked for burial in the Gilbertine house at Sempringham, and one at the Praemonstratensian canonry at Hales Owen. We have seen that the monasteries attracted but few chantries, though they were a popular choice for burial. Endowments to them usually took the form of prayers said by all the brethren, rather than by a few men committed to a special interest, as in a chantry. But if monasteries resented the intrusion of a chantry, they certainly did not mind being drawn out of their set routine by the pleasant excitement of a funeral. Neither did they mind accepting the obligations that went with receiving bodies for burial, if their continuous popularity is any criterion.

The Mendicants enjoyed some small distinction as hosts for burials. Of the wills analysed, 15 per cent expressed a desire for burial in a friary church. The four major orders shared the thirty burials: the Carmelites had four, as did the Austin Friars. Seven Franciscan houses received nine people; two were houses of Franciscan minoresses. Seven Dominican houses received twelve peers—two each at Stamford, Worcester, and Oxford, and three in the London Blackfriars. In contrast to the friaries, cathedral churches were not a major burial place for the nobles, though their attraction might seem obvious, particularly to people apt to spend lavishly on their funerals and tombs. York was the most popular cathedral, but this was because the Scropes of Masham rested there. No burials at all are recorded for Lincoln, Winchester, or Hereford. Perhaps the nobles did not flock to the cathedrals because they could not hope to over-awe those great houses of worship. Jealous bishops may not have welcomed the secular peerage. Whatever the reason, the cathedrals were neither well-endowed nor a popular place of burial. Bishops, deans, abbots, and kings stand as the great cathedral builders of medieval England, rather than the secular peers.

When all the parish churches of the realm are counted, the number of secular institutions is at least ten times that of the regular houses. So it is no wonder that so many nobles chose secular establishments for burial. But on the other hand, when their importance and wealth qualified them for a more august home, burial in a local church is evidence of the strength of local feeling. The nobleman often preferred to be the major figure, in death as in life, within a small world revolving around himself, his family, and his immediate circle. The local church or chapel was overwhelmed by his eternal presence, as the cathedral or conventual church was not. And many a peer did have genuine affection for the church he had supported and in which he, often in company with numerous ancestors, had worshipped over the years.

But our basic interest here is in what the nobles gave to the places of their burial, rather than simply in classifying sites. We seek patterns of burial and of burial-house endowment. Not all wills that stipulated the place of burial even left bequests to that church. But the majority did, leaving gifts in a variety of forms. The simplest way of enriching the burial house was by simple bequest; an outright gift in cash or kind, sometimes in property yet to be alienated. Mortmain grants were not so frequently made in the wills, as they had to be supervised and followed up, while gifts in kind could be handed over almost immediately. The objects given were usually vestments and robes, chapel furnishings and furniture, chalices, plate, candelabra and the like, i.e. possessions of religious use and value. And as they came from a peer's private chapel, we may assume they frequently were of aesthetic interest and with some intrinsic value. Such objects were given to the burial house itself, rather than to any of its members, in contrast to the practice of leaving sums to each separate resident of the favoured institution. When a monastery benefited from this latter form of bequest, the sums for the abbot or prior were invariably greater than those for simple monks or canons.

Men requesting burial in Benedictine conventual churches usually came with ample endowments, mostly in the form of personal possessions. John Warrenne ordered that the six horses from his funeral procession were to become property of St Pancras, Lewes.[1] Edward Despenser gave vestments, chalices, and a ewer in which to put 'the body of Christ' on Corpus Christi day.[2] Richard Scrope left his vestments, albs, chalices, candelabra, etc., to the house of St Agatha, Richmond, a favourite burial house within his family.[3] John Neville left his 'magnum missale' as mortuary, along with two candlesticks, to St Mary, York.[4] The Countess of Warwick bequeathed her wedding gown to Tewkesbury, along with the ornaments and plate from her private chapel.[5] As the peer's chapel was frequently dismantled after his death, its valuable furnishings and sacramental equipment were an attractive plum for a fortunate church. Books, owned by nobles in fair numbers in this period, if not in great variety, were included among the gifts in kind. Humphrey Stafford left Abbotsbury a missal, 'unum portiforium vocatum magnum ligger ... secundum usum Saresburiensem', along with vestments and chapel ornaments, the mere enumeration of which takes almost a page in the printed version of his will.[6]

Straight cash bequests were less commonly made. St Agatha at Richmond received £40 as mortuary from Richard Scrope.[7] Richard FitzAlan's bequest of £200 to the monks of Lewes, with which to buy land and rents, was for the perpetual support of a two-man chantry.[8] Elizabeth Stafford left but £4 3s 4d to Tewkesbury.[9] Stephen Scrope left 20 marks, again for the support of prayers, to St Agatha's,[10] and Richard Scrope gave that house £10 in gold.[11] Thomas Beaufort bequeathed 200 marks to Bury, for anniversary masses for his soul.[12] Hingham Abbey received 6s 8d for the enrichment of the high altar from Isabella Morley, plus £2 for general repairs.[13] Though most

[1] *TE*, I, 42.
[2] *TV*, p. 99.
[3] *TE*, I, 274.
[4] *TE*, II, 7.
[5] *TV*, p. 240.
[6] Jacob, p. 621.
[7] *TE*, I, 329.
[8] *TV*, p. 94.
[9] *TV*, p. 172.
[10] *TE*, III, 38.
[11] *TV*, p. 201.
[12] Jacob, p. 356.
[13] Blomefield: *History of Norfolk*, II, 430.

bequests to the burial house had prayers as their end, the explicit request for services is frequently found in the will when the bequest was in cash but not so often when it took the form of a gift of personal possessions. A cash bequest was more blatantly a business transaction.

When the will made provision for cash disbursements to each monk in a house, these were rarely large. The 13s 4d which Richard Scrope left for each man at St Agatha could not have been a heavy burden upon his estate.[14] Richard's son left another 6s 8d per monk when he died three years later.[15] The Scrope family lavished constant attention on this Richmondshire house; such a tradition was by no means rare. Nobles might leave cash bequests with mundane conditions attached. The abbot, if present when Thomas Beaufort was buried at Bury, was to receive 6s 8d, the prior 3s 4d, and each monk but 1s 8d.[16] Beaufort left £400 in cash to the house as a corporation, and an equal or larger sum to other houses, so we do not get the impression that he was spoiling the monks, irregular though the practice of individual bequests may have been. Humphrey Stafford left only 1s per monk of Glastonbury who prayed for him on the day of his funeral, and 8d per servant of the house then present.

In so far as it is possible to compare burial bequests left to Benedictine and Austin houses, we can say that the Black Monks profited more per bequest. Only the Austin canonry at Bisham was an exception, because of the great Montague benefactions. Otherwise Austin houses received less per burial, despite their great popularity. Bequests of goods were less frequently made to them, and those made were apt to be quite modest. William Latimer left all the beasts of his manor of Ugthorpe, plus jewels, chapel utensils, and a cape for each canon of Guisborough.[17] But this was unwonted generosity. Isabel Fauconberg simply left the 'best' beast at her death.[18] Edmund Mortimer was another exception, for he left to his favourite house at Wigmore a 'large cross of gold set with stones, with a relique of the cross of Our Lord, a bone of St Richard the Confessor, Bishop of Chichester, and the Finger of St Thomas de Cantelowe, Bishop of Hereford, and the reliques of St Thomas of Canterbury'.[19] Relics

[14] *TE*, I, 274.
[15] *TE*, I, 329.
[16] Jacob, p. 356.
[17] *TE*, I, 113–14.
[18] *TE*, I, 282.
[19] *TV*, p. 111.

were not usually allowed to stray outside the family fortunate enough to possess them.

Cash did come to Austin houses, both in lump sums and in *per capita* allocations. Margaret Scrope left £1 to the prior of Christ Church, London, 13s 4d for the sub-prior, 6s 8d per canon, and 3s 4d for each unordained clerk.[20] The identical hierarchy of payments was ordered by others.[21] William Latimer left £2 for an annual obit for himself, and £20 to cover the cost of his tomb and the purchase of a missal and vestments.[22] Thomas Neville gave Worksop Priory £40 for the fabric of the church and a campanile, the bequests to be paid either in cash or in the equivalent value in lead.[23] Anne Stafford turned 100 marks over to Llanthony by Gloucester.[24] Bisham Priory received huge sums in cash: 400 marks for the chantry of Elizabeth Montague in 1415, £40 for her funeral expenses, 100 marks for her tomb, £20 for vestments for the canons, etc: 500 marks from the Earl of Salisbury in 1429 for his tomb,[25] and comparable sums for other Montagues and Nevilles. But different people had different ideas of value for their money: Walter FitzWalter left 40 marks for his burial services and ceremonies to Dunmow, but only £2 to the prior and canons for prayers.[26] Hugh Stafford wanted 500 masses within a year of burial. This must have meant a good bit of money for Stone Priory,[27] though we have seen how wide a range of bequests and generosity might be encompassed. It is unsafe to speculate whether the house received £2 or £50 for the prayers.

Other orders did not do as well. The mendicants got cash from those buried in their churches, not personal possessions. Peter Mauley's gift of a beast to the Doncaster Franciscans,[28] and Elizabeth Bohun's miscellaneous bequests of books, clothes, bells, a silver pot, and a 'cross made of the very wood of Our Saviour's Cross which I was wont to carry about with me, and wherein is contained one of the thorns of His crown',[29] are exceptions. More in keeping with the

[20] *TE*, IV, 4.
[21] Among them, Beatrice Roos to Warter Priory, *TE*, I, 376, and Matilda Montague, PCC, Luffenham 2.
[22] *TE*, I, 113–14.
[23] *TE*, III, 41.
[24] Dugdale: *Baronage*, I, 164.
[25] Jacob, pp. 15, 397.
[26] Jacob, p. 469.
[27] *TV*, p. 118.
[28] *TE*, I, 117.
[29] *TV*, p. 60.

usual practice was Maud Say's gifts of £10 to the London Dominic-ans.[30] Lady Ida St Amand's £2 to the Oxford Franciscans, and John de Montfort's £10 to the Warwick Dominicans were typical.[31] There were also some large grants. John Beauchamp left 40 marks for the repair of the Dominican house at Worcester, where the friars men-tioned him by name daily. He also left 20 marks for his funeral, 8*d* per week for masses, and 2*d* per day for food, 'augmentyng and emendyng of ther far and diete'.[32] We have seen other instances of the pious generosity of Elizabeth Burgh. She was buried in the London Minoresses, to whom she bequeathed £20 in cash, numerous jewels and vestments, £20 for the abbess, 13*s* 4*d* per sister on the day of her funeral, and 10 marks to the four friars attached to the house.[33] Lord Say left £100 to the London Grey Friars, largely to be expended on the 4,000 masses he wanted said within six weeks of his demise.[34] Those who chose burial in a friary church seem to have had confid-ence that wishes would be honoured and money well used.

Since they often ordered elaborate and attractive tombs, the nobles must take some blame for the splendour of the mendicant churches. Hugh Despenser gave orders for the enlargement of his uncle's chapel in the Dominican church at Stamford, and he provided marble stones for himself, his wife, and his parents.[35] John Beauchamp's benefactions to the Worcester Dominicans included a lime and stone chapel, as he called it, and to be built in goodly haste and in accordance with an indenture made with one John Hobbes, a Gloucester mason. The chapel was to include an alabaster image of its main occupant.[36] His wife elaborated the details of the alabaster tablet, which was to depict 'the Birth of Our Lord; and the three kings of Coleyn', while a second image was to be of John the Evangelist, 'containing 3 quarter of a yard in length, with the chalice in his hand'.[37]

If Humphrey Bohun gave the London Austin Friars but little in his will, all concerned remembered that he had virtually refounded the house less than a decade before his death.[38] In contrast to this was the ostentatious behaviour of Thomas Bromflete, buried in the London

[30] *TV*, p. 83.
[31] Dugdale: *Baronage*, II, 21; I, 411.
[32] PCC, Logge 13.
[33] *RW*, pp. 23–30.
[34] *TV*, p. 264.
[35] Gibbons: pp. 98–9.
[36] PCC, Logge 13.
[37] Dugdale: *Baronage*, I, 250.
[38] *RW*, p. 44; Dugdale: *Baronage*, I, 185.

Carmelite house. Though Dugdale hails him, 'of all that Order throughout England, he thereby expresseth that he was principal Founder', he left no bequest to his burial house, and did not even say that the six chaplain chantry he endowed was to be put there.[39] We do know that his executors built a single chaplain chantry at Beverley. Such gratuitous neglect was also practised by Thomas Ughtred, who wished to be buried beside his wife in the Franciscan house at York, but who left his money to the other mendicant houses there.[40] There must have been an earlier benefaction in this and similar cases. Ughtred might well have made his when he buried his wife, a few years earlier.

Cathedrals profited more from the chantries and tombs they hosted than from generous gifts accompanying burial. The £140 which the Earl of Pembroke left to St Paul's was for a tomb, to be constructed like that of Elizabeth Burgh in the Minories;[41] hers must have enjoyed considerable fame. The Hungerford endowments to Salisbury Cathedral were, likewise, tied quite closely to their own chantries, though Lord Walter left £10 to be distributed among the cathedral clergy at his funeral, 'in the customary manner'.[42] Stephen Scrope endowed a chantry at York and left 20 marks towards the construction of the choir there, in progress at the time of his death.[43] Ralph Neville made the most generous burial grant to a cathedral when he gave Durham vestments, his four best horses (valued in his will at 100 marks), hundreds of pounds of wax, £120 for repairs to the church fabric, tunics, stoles, books, and £1 per monk, up to £50.[44] Such munificence was extraordinary, and his bequests were not weighed down with specific reciprocal obligations or construction projects. Most cathedral clerics would consider themselves fortunate if the 5s 4d per canon, offered those at John Scrope's funeral, was promptly paid.[45] The distinction between enriching the house and its separate residents must be constantly borne in mind.

Secular establishments drew about the same support as did regular ones in this regard, i.e. there usually was some bequest, but the spectrum of endowments ranged very widely, from near-neglect to

[39] Dugdale: *Baronage*, II, 234.
[40] *TE*, I, 242.
[41] *TV*, p. 87.
[42] *TV*, p. 257.
[43] *TE*, III, 32.
[44] *Wills and Inventories*, pp. 26–7.
[45] *TE*, II, 186.

sums which would almost have rebuilt the house. There is no indication that a man who desired burial in a cathedral or conventual
church had to be prepared to pay more for that privilege than one
who chose a humble parish church. Neither, conversely, is there
reason to think that those who would pay more chose to be buried in
a grander institution. Bequests of personal possessions were commonly made to secular colleges, and they were of much the same nature
as those presented to regular houses. Beasts went, as mortuary payments. Robert Willoughby's best horse and best saddle came to his
foundation at Spilsby, 'in satisfaction of tithes and obligations forgotten or negligently paid by me'.[46] John Greystoke left his horse and
arms to Greystoke college.[47] He and Willoughby chose to be buried
in establishments they had favoured in life. Personal possessions were
left in such unordered profusion that there can be no summary of
them. That a nobleman could enumerate so many separate items of
his wardrobe and chapel is a testimonial to the frequency with which
he used them, and possibly to the avarice with which he had inherited
or collected them. William Hastings left a jewel worth £20, by his
own assessment, to St George's chapel, Windsor.[48] Thomas Beauchamp bequeathed 300 pounds of wax to Our Lady, Warwick, and
his son Richard gave a pure gold image to that house.[49] St Katherine
by the Tower received a jewelled cup, a chalice, vestments, etc., from
John Holland.[50] The most precious gift was the cross Elizabeth
Willoughby gave to Spilsby: 'in which is a piece of the cross of Our
Lord, and set with 2 rubies and 2 emeralds, and a circle of pearls on
the head; to remain there forever, without being alienated.'[51] The
presence of the last qualification makes us wonder how much faith
the nobles had in some of their beneficiaries.

Cash came in frequently to the secular houses. Our Lady, Warwick,
received many such bequests from the Beauchamps and the Nevilles,
including the sums needed for the fourteenth century rebuilding. Earl
Richard left land worth £40, for a chantry.[52] Jane Neville left 10
marks in cash, Elizabeth Neville £10 in land (i.e. in land returning £10

[46] *TV*, p. 136.
[47] *TE*, I, 85–6.
[48] *TV*, p. 369.
[49] *TV*, pp. 154, 231.
[50] *TV*, p. 255.
[51] Gibbons, p. 91.
[52] *TV*, p. 231.

cash per annum).[53] These people also left numerous personal possessions. Ralph Cromwell left money to his foundation at Tattershall,[54]
and William Botreaux was a conscientious founder of North Cadbury
to the very end.[55]

More nobles were buried in parish churches than in colleges. The
churches frequently got something as mortuary. A horse, perhaps
with the bridle and the owner's arms, was a common form of this
payment, and some peers were good enough to specify that it was to
be the best horse. Other bequests of goods were as seen above. The
church at Staverdale was lucky enough to get a silver cup, 'quod fuit
sancti Thome Martiris'.[56] Most gifts were more prosaic, and we encounter many bequests of vestments and similar goods, for every
souvenir of Becket's household that was still in circulation. Books
were often found in the lists of items given. Robert Roos was hardly
exceptional either in his literacy or his generosity when he gave a
missal, two portiforia, and a gradual to the church at Ingmanthorp.[57]
Lady Clinton passed her new 'masseboke' on to Haversham church.[58]

Cash was left to parish churches either to pay for prayers or else
for the fabric. The sums left varied from the 400 marks of Michael
and Joan Poynings, for construction at Poynings church,[59] to the £2
which Richard Grey of Wilton bequeathed for the high altar of
Bletchley church.[60] Certainly, numerous bequests for purposes of
construction were specifically directed when parish churches were the
recipients. As well as money for general building purposes, there were
also many bequests for the decoration of the high altar and its furnishings. Philip Bardolf covered both categories, leaving 5 marks for
the altar of Dennington church, and another £5 for repairs to the
fabric.[61] When burial was in a parish church, a higher percentage of
all the total bequests went to institutions other than the burial house.
Parish churches did not attract the great number of costly tombs. But
the needs (or demands) of a parish church were less insatiable, so less
money was likely to be tied up in a single complicated bequest to

[53] *North Country Wills*, p. 55; *TV*, p. 359.
[54] *TE*, II, 197.
[55] *TV*, p. 191.
[56] *Somerset Wills*, p. 144.
[57] *TE*, I, 179.
[58] Jacob, p. 266.
[59] Dugdale: *Baronage*, II, 134.
[60] Jacob, p. 627.
[61] *Ibid.*, p. 602.

them. But they usually did quite well, considering that almost any nobleman's bequest would have represented appreciable help in a world where £5 or less could support a parish priest.

Sometimes we can find family traditions of endowment to burial churches, though we never have information on more than a few members of any family. Those which actively supported or helped to build a church can be assumed to have had a predilection towards substantial bequests to that house if they chose it as a burial site (as most founders did).[62] We have seen that members of a family prayed for each other, and it was only natural in a society which believed in bodily resurrection that they would choose to lie together in those churches where the prayers were often being said. The Beauchamps offer illustrative data. They did not have a *de novo* foundation to their credit, but they spent vast sums on St Mary, Warwick, and it was very properly seen as their church. The two Earls Thomas, with wills respectively from 1369 and 1400, and Earl Richard, with a will from 1435, were all buried there. Each man endowed the church, via a testamentary bequest, and each called for a funeral of some grandeur, as well as for a large number of prayers to be said shortly after death. The first Earl Thomas left 500 marks for his funeral, plus instructions and money for a new choir.[63] His successor made provision for a large funeral procession; 30 trentals, and 1,000 masses.[64] Earl Richard asked to be laid near his father, once the chapel for them had been completed.[65] But all three men left these bequests in the context of wills containing many other bequests, to many other beneficiaries. Only a small part of their total bequests went to the burial house.

Furthermore, these Beauchamps were not the entire family. Earl Richard's wife chose to be buried, not at St Mary, but at Tewkesbury, a site favoured by her own ancestors, the Despensers. She left extensive bequests to her burial house, so the monks would 'groche nogt with my lyenge'. Her will contained no bequests at all for St Mary's.[66] And though the Beauchamps had been connected with the college for centuries, earlier earls had not been buried there, nor did they always leave bequests in their wills. Earl Guy had asked in 1315 to be buried

[62] Susan Wood: *English Monasteries and Their Patrons in the Thirteenth Century* (Oxford, 1955), pp. 129–30.
[63] *TV*, p. 79.
[64] *TV*, p. 154.
[65] *TV*, p. 231.
[66] *Fifty Earliest English Wills*, p. 116.

at Bordesley.[67] Others rested elsewhere: Roger at the Fishton Black Friars, Lord St Amand at Steeple Lavington, and Lord Powicke and his wife at the Worcester Dominican house.[68] None of these Beauchamp cousins remembered the Warwick church in their wills. As in life, the family was scattered in death. When the Nevilles took over the Beauchamp traditions, Jane and Elizabeth Neville asked to be buried in the chapel of Our Lady, Warwick. Elizabeth, daughter of the last Beauchamp earl, was to be laid between her father, her son, and her son-in-law.[69] Jane was to lie beside her husband Henry, son of Lord Latimer.[70] Elizabeth left money for a chantry, vestments, and images to grace four family graves there. Jane left vestments as well as 10 marks cash, to cover three years' worth of prayers by a chantry priest.

In the fourteenth century the Nevilles had had numerous ties with Durham cathedral, and their wills bear out this affiliation. Lord Ralph Neville left much of his personal property and cash to that church, and John Neville asked for a sumptuous funeral and burial there, next to his wife, a daughter of Henry Percy.[71] But other members of the family followed other inclinations. Lord Latimer was buried at St Mary, York, only bequeathing a missal and a few ornaments to Durham.[72] Lord Furnivall, brother to the Earl of Westmorland, asked to lie at Worksop, which priory he had enriched with a £40 cash bequest, plus any residue after a funeral which was to be without pomp.[73] Sir John Neville asked for burial at Haltemprice, in the Wake family's Austin canonry. He left that house a courser, vestments, chalices, and 10 marks for one year's worth of chantry prayers.[74]

In 1458 the Earl of Salisbury asked for burial at Bisham, a house of his in-laws, the Montagues. He bequeathed some £400 for a tomb, a funeral, and prayers there. But with these vast endowments he was buying himself a place beside his wife's illustrious relatives.[75] His unusual generosity was so that he could be identified as a Montague, it

[67] *TV*, p. 54.
[68] PCC, Marche 86; *TV*, p. 281; Dugdale: *Baronage*, I, 250; PCC, Logge 13.
[69] *TV*, p. 358.
[70] *North Country Wills*, p. 55.
[71] *Wills and Inventories*, pp. 26–7, 38.
[72] *TE*, II, 7.
[73] *TE*, III, 41.
[74] *TV*, p. 265.
[75] *TV*, pp. 286–7.

would seem, rather than as a Neville. To what extent was the choice of the burial site and of the size of the accompanying endowment matters of general family concern? An examination of the habits of some families furthers the view that while one was free to go as one chose, one was hardly encouraged to begin an endless cycle of new family traditions regarding burial sites and the accompanying burial-house bequests.

The Montague line had once been quite loyal to its house at Bisham. The founder, his son William, his countess, and Thomas Montague were all buried there. Their gifts have already been discussed; each left sums of cash for his funeral, plus money for the fabric of the house and for the separate canons. They were steadfast in supporting Bisham, and they had no other pet projects to distract them or to divert their benefactions.

The Scropes of Bolton likewise showed this sort of provincialism, as they went to burial at St Agatha Richmond. Between 1400 and 1420 four of them chose the house, and all brought bequests of some value. Richard, in 1400, left £40 to the abbot, 13s 4d per canon, and innumerable goods and articles of clothing. Roger gave £40 as mortuary, plus 6s 8d in cash to each canon. Stephen came accompanied by fewer bequests, but Richard, in 1420, laid extensive (if abortive) plans for a college of five priests, five clerks, and three poor men, adjacent to the convent.[76] Only Margaret Scrope asked to be buried in Holy Trinity, London, and she bequeathed just a few pounds' cash to her burial house, to be divided among the residents.[77] She broke the family traditions of both place of burial and of munificent burial bequests. The Scropes of Masham parted company with their cousins, and were buried in their chapel, 'vulgarieter vocata Scrop Chapell' in York Minster.[78] John Scrope built the chapel, and he left 2s per canon, 3s 4d to each one saying a requiem mass, and 1s to other participants, 1s per vicar, 6d per deacon, and 4d per chorister: plus small cash payments, jewels, and a chantry to be built from any residue of his estate.[79] His father had left 20 marks for work on the choir, plus cash for two chantries, one to last for a year, with the priest getting 13s 4d as an outright gift, and a rather minimal four marks for the year of service. The other chantry was to be supported

[76] *TE*, I, 273–4, 328–9; *TE*, III, 38; *TV*, p. 201.
[77] *TE*, IV, 4.
[78] *TE*, II, 186.
[79] *TE*, II, 185–9.

from any residue of his estate after debts and bequests had been paid. It was for two old and honest priests, at 10 marks per annum, at St Stephen's altar.[80]

In some cases there is nothing approaching a strong family tradition of common burial site. The FitzAlans had favoured the Cluniac Priory at Lewes until they transferred their allegiance to their own college at Arundel. Earl Richard left £200 for the monks at Lewes, for the purchase of land and rents, and for the maintenance of a perpetual chantry, plus 50 marks for his funeral, and an unspecified sum for a tomb near that of his wife.[81] But the fifteenth-century tradition was of burial at Arundel.[82] Earl Thomas left £133 6s 8d to the secular college, 'pro exequiis meis faciendis tam pro aliis funeralibus missis celebrandis quam elemosinis et operibus caritatis'.[83] Countess Joan left £40 in cash, and the customary vestments to the college.[84] Countess Elizabeth, buried there with her husband, left £40 for an annual obit, plus 200 marks for a chantry, to be maintained for twenty years or more, at the altar of Our Lady.[85]

Three of the Willoughbys of Eresby were buried at Spilsby College within a relatively short period: Lady Margaret in 1359, Elizabeth in 1394, and Robert in 1395. None left any appreciable bequests to their burial house. It may be a case of few burial bequests because of generosity in life—we know the family had tried to establish a college in the church. Or do we have here an example of a family where some went, without many accompanying bequests of their own, to a house to which the family had once given large endowments, while others just turned their backs and went off elsewhere? There are numerous other families with several burials in one church. Most of them left endowments of respectable size, but some did not. It is hard to generalize, and there is no way of knowing why a peer did or did not enrich the house in which he requested burial.

The greater the interval between the deaths the less likelihood of a common burial site for the members of a family. Traditions binding people within one generation were likely to weaken through the course of a century. Six Staffords were buried in five different churches in about

[80] *TE*, III, 32–7.
[81] *TV*, p. 94.
[82] *RW*, pp. 120–5, for a transitional will: burial at Lewes, but more bequests actually going to Arundel.
[83] Jacob, p. 74.
[84] Jacob, p. 541.
[85] *TV*, p. 277.

a century, and yet each indicated some generosity to his chosen site. Earl Humphrey, in 1385, was laid to rest in Stone priory, with his wife. He endowed prayers there, but made no other bequests. They might have been made when his wife had been buried, when prayers for both of them had begun.[86] In 1405 Elizabeth Stafford was buried at Abbotsbury, rejoining her husband.[87] Prayers and cash accompanied her. In 1439 Anne Stafford was buried at Llanthony by Gloucester, in a tomb she had already had built. She bequeathed a further 100 marks to her burial house.[88] In 1442 Humphrey was buried at Abbotsbury, leaving books, ornaments, vestments, images, etc.[89] His son, in a will of 1463, asked to be buried at Glastonbury, a place of great holiness but of no other Staffords. Though most of his will was devoted to a detailed confession of his sins, he did leave some cash for the house, and a small sum for the monks.[90] Lastly, Anne, duchess of Buckingham, in 1480 requested burial at Pleshey College, a royal foundation in Essex.[91] The Staffords generally endowed whatever house they chose for burial, but had no traditional site for interment. They implicitly accepted one common pattern of behaviour and ignored the more diverse one practised by families like the Beauchamps and the Montagues.

But the spread of years did not invariably mean the separation of a family. In 1368 William Ferrers asked to be buried at Ulverscroft, leaving £100 to the poor and for funeral expenses.[92] In 1410 Elizabeth Ferrers was buried in Holy Cross, London. She left money for the church's fabric, plus prayers.[93] But then, in 1445, William Ferrers requested burial at Ulverscroft again[94]. So families did occasionally honour an old tradition. The whole system of prayers for the dead would have served to remind people of where their ancestors were buried, and churches were usually ready to welcome noble funerals and tombs.

Some peers were buried in houses to which they left no testamentary bequests. In some cases we know that the individual or his family

---

[86] *TV*, p. 118.
[87] *TV*, p. 166.
[88] Dugdale: *Baronage*, I, 164.
[89] Jacob, pp. 620–2.
[90] *Somerset Wills*, p. 196.
[91] *TV*, pp. 356–7.
[92] *TV*, p. 76.
[93] PCC, Marche, 198b.
[94] Dugdale: *Baronage*, I, 269.

had a previous connection with the church. In 1372 Humphrey Bohun asked to be buried in Walden Abbey, and he vaguely left them the residue of his goods.[95] But in 1343 he had alienated the manor and advowson of Berdon to Walden.[96] The Despensers had a tie with Tewkesbury Abbey. Edward was buried there, and yet his will only bequeathed some ornaments and a few personal possessions.[97] But some years before Hugh Despenser had alienated land and the advowson of Llantrissam to the house.[98] Other instances are not hard to find, and they indicate the existence of long-standing family ties, not indicated in the wills. A man might choose to leave his gifts before his death; he had more control over the process then, and he might enjoy the prestige he gained. Thus while many wills indicate no bequests to the house of burial, it cannot be assumed that the peer in question was simply instructing his executors to leave his body, and nothing else, in a church which was under no particular obligation to him, and which was to receive nothing but the standard mortuary fees.

Some nobles did not specify the place of burial, but left the choice up to their executors. Since these testators had little idea of where they would lie, they understandably had little proprietorial feeling for the unknown church. The bequests in such wills are usually for prayers, bought with cash, rather than for gifts of goods and personal items for the maintenance of the church's fabric or residents. Constance Straunge was to be buried wherever it pleased her husband, and the £5 she bequeathed was for 200 masses, with *placebo* and *dirige*.[99] John Scrope left vestments to his family's beloved York Minster, but his burial was to be whosesoever God pleased.[100] This pattern was repeated in the case of Lucy Holland. Though Bourne Abbey, a favourite house of hers, was to get 1,000 crowns, she did not specify burial there, beside her husband: 'my body to be buried wheresoever it please God'.[101] Guy Beauchamp, son of the Earl of Warwick, asked to be buried 'where my parents think proper'.[102] His mother, when her turn came, obligingly asked for burial where her husband thought fit.[103] Some of these indecisive people left no pro-

[95] *TV*, p. 89.
[96] *CPR 1343–45*, p. 62.
[97] *TV*, p. 99.
[98] *CPR 1343–45*, p. 118.
[99] *TV*, p. 235.
[100] *TE*, I, 339.
[101] *TV*, p. 205.
[102] *TV*, p. 631.
[103] Dugdale: *Baronage*, I, 234.

visions for any bequests, but others gave a good deal to specific beneficiaries.

There is also a group of nobles who named several places in which the burial might take place. As the variable was usually where death would occur, the practice of making the will when close to death restricted the number of such people. Still, in anything as eccentric as testamentary disposition, almost any possibility will be covered by a few individuals. James Audley is typical of them: to be buried in 'my' abbey of Hilton if he dies on the Welsh Marches, at the Exeter Dominican house if in Devon or Somerset.[104] In either case, Hilton was to get a bequest of £10 for prayers. The only other bequests in his will were for funeral expenses, and the Dominicans would only profit if they actually got the body. Perhaps other benefactions had been made or would be offered if he did die in the south-west. He did not appear to consider the possibility of dying elsewhere—an indication of how localized even an aristocrat's life might be.

Anne Mautravers covered herself against all eventualities. If she died in Dorset or Wiltshire, she was to lie in the church of Our Lady, Lychet Mautravers; if death came while she was in Hertfordshire or Cambridge, then in Wymondley priory. Regardless, Lychet Mautravers was to get £2 in cash, and Wymondley her persona lsilver, after her son's death.[105] It is sometimes hard to know on what basis the ultimate choice was made. Ralph Neville wanted burial either in Durham Cathedral or in Staindrop college.[106] Sometimes perhaps the man could not make up his mind, and others were left with the decision when he was past caring. But in other instances the concern with burial did not even end with death. Thomas FitzAlan asked to be buried in Edessdon church, with reinterment in the Dorchester Franciscan house when his debts were fully paid.[107] Most nobles were explicit, however, and most said burial was to be within the church, rather than in the churchyard.

We have seen the great variation in the quantity and quality of goods a noble would bring with him to his burial house. What proportion of all testamentary bequests went to that church? Bequests to the burial house were of both a secular nature, e.g. horses and armour, choice items of furniture, etc., and of a sacred nature, e.g. chapel

[104] *TV*, p. 117.
[105] *TV*, p. 92.
[106] *TE*, I, 69–73.
[107] *TV*, p. 378.

H   99

ornaments, ecclesiastical vestments, relics, prayer books, etc. Though the nobles rarely gave all their personal possessions to their burial house, they rarely gave more than one or two of these personal items to any ecclesiastical house other than that chosen as a burial site. Goods which did not accompany the body usually stayed within the family or went to a trusted friend or servant. Obviously, a generalization which embraces thousands of bequests does not hold in every case, but usually other religious houses, when remembered, got bequests in cash, rather than in objects of sentimental or intrinsic value.

How much cash did the other churches get, in terms of the percentage of the value of all ecclesiastically directed bequests? Again, the answer admits of great variation. Sometimes a will only made provision for bequests to the burial house. Others ignore that church, and leave all relevant bequests to other religious foundations. If we divide the realm of recipients into two, burial sites and all others, it is to be expected that in absolute terms most wills left a majority of bequests to institutions other than the burial church. But this is an unfair bifurcation. Ordinarily a man was buried in but one place, while there was no limit to the number he could endow *in absentia*. The crucial point is that the burial house usually came in for a larger share of the bequests than any other single church named on the will. On the shorter wills, where fewer houses were named, the endowments to the burial house usually represented a good fraction, perhaps 20 to 25 per cent of all the ecclesiastical endowments, both in number and value. When money spent on the funeral is also considered, the burial house often attracted about half of what many a peer had to give to the church in his will, with the rest of the bequests perhaps being scattered among a dozen or more different recipients. Little has been said about the tombs the nobles ordered for themselves, but many were quite sumptuous, and the burial house stood to profit still further from these. So the conclusion must be that a church stood to profit handsomely when it was chosen by a nobleman for his burial.

A geographical survey of burials sheds a little light, for most people chose to be buried near a major residence. That the Nevilles sometimes chose Durham cathedral, the Scropes various Yorkshire churches, the Berkeleys the Bristol Austin canonry, the Mortimers Wigmore, etc., is what we expect. But there is another side to this coin. That is provided by the large number of burials and burial endowments in London. Because members of the peerage were so provincial in their lands and wealth, the concentration of their physical remains in the churches of the city is striking. Their chantry endowments in London were out of proportion to their level of alienations. The exceptional popularity of London as a burial site confirms the view that, while they felt little affinity for London in the ordinary course of their lives, the approach of death turned noble thoughts towards the great metropolis.

The mendicant houses were particularly popular. Humphrey Bohun, rebuilder of the London Austin Friary, was buried there in 1361. Beyond what he spent during his life, he left money for prayers and for distribution to fifty friars, for his soul's sake.[108] Elizabeth Bohun chose the Dominican house, and left it 100 marks, a relic cross, cloth, books, etc.[109] Maud Say, who left them £10, and Richard Scrope, also leaving £10, were likewise buried at Blackfriars.[110] Lord Vescy left £10 to the Carmelite house which accepted his remains.[111] James Fiennes left £100 to the Franciscans, for a funeral and prayer services (4,000 masses within six weeks of his death), and John Blount left £20.[112] Elizabeth Burgh and Anne Hastings both requested burial in the Minoresses church: Agnes left 20 marks and a pair of silver candlesticks.[113] Elizabeth, though actually buried at Ware, left £20 to the London nuns, plus vestments, jewels, £20 to the abbess, and 13s 4d per sister.[114] Most nobles buried in London left generous endowments. John Holland left 80 marks, plus jewels, books, and personal belongings. He was buried beside his wife and sister in St Katherine's.[115] John Hastings wanted his tomb in St Paul's to resemble that of Elizabeth de Burgh, and he left £140 for it, plus another £200 for two chantry priests.[116] Other wills tell a similar story—both for burial within the city and for such as Joan Cobham, buried at St Mary Overy, Southwark, and Margaret de la Pole, buried in St Saviour's, Bermondsey.[117] One did not go to London for burial without bringing a respectable offering, and many nobles thought the price well worth paying.

[108] *RW*, pp. 44–7.
[109] *TV*, p. 60.
[110] *TV*, p. 83; *TE*, III, 298.
[111] PCC, Godyn 215b.
[112] *TV*, p. 264; *TV*, 386.
[113] *TV*, p. 72.
[114] *RW*, pp. 23–31.
[115] *RW*, pp. 282–3.
[116] *RW*, pp. 92–4.
[117] *TV*, pp. 81, 328.

6

⤜◇◇⤛

Miscellaneous philanthropy

⤜◇◇⤛

SOME forms of philanthropic activity are almost impossible to study in a systematic fashion. We have not investigated the daily distribution of alms, nor the random endowments and benefactions made by means other than alienations in mortmain or testamentary bequests. We know that the distribution of alms through the household officials was a regular part of an aristocrat's life.[1] We know a good deal about how alms were distributed by the royal household and in a few noble households. Except that smaller quantities were involved, there is every reason to assume that the average noble household functioned in a similar way, and that food, clothing, and cash were distributed regularly. If the royal household gave out hundreds of pounds in goods and money each year, and John of Gaunt averaged at least £50–75, we would expect the typical noble to hand out at least £10–20, and some to rise well above this figure.[2] But apart from random references, the sources for such information are lost, scattered, and unculled. So, important though the role of such random charity should be in assessing the philanthropy of the nobility, it cannot yet be dealt with.

Casual gifts and endowments are even harder to deal with. As well as alms to the poor at their door, during the course of their lives the nobles gave money and possessions to numerous ecclesiastical

---

[1] 'In the house of a lord, after every meal a basket filled with fragments of food not eaten was taken to the poor at the gate.' F. Harrison: *Medieval Man and His Notions* (London, 1947), p. 101.

[2] Hilda Johnstone: 'Poor Relief in the Royal Household of 13th Century England', *Speculum*, IV (1926), pp. 149–67. For the office of royal almoner A. R. Myers: *The Household of Edward IV* (Manchester, 1959), *passim*; *John of Gaunt's Register*, S. Armitage-Smith (ed.), Camden Society, 3rd series, xxi (1911).

institutions. Some of the recipient institutions housed relatives, friends, or old servants, and they looked to the head of the great local family for extra support. Some houses were simply neighbours, able to impress the local peer with their need and merit. How often the nobles were moved to make such contributions we cannot even guess. Many of the bequests in wills may have been follow-up grants, coming after bequests made in life. But this type of activity is not controlled through its recorded appearance in a single type of source. Consequently, we concentrate in this chapter on certain aspects of charity and endowment found in the wills. They at least can be isolated.

Only a small proportion of noble wills call for the distribution of alms, either at the time of death or at some future point. By 'alms' we mean bequests made to unnamed and usually unknown individuals, e.g. the poor, or 'the paupers at my funeral'. We do not include grants made to the regular or secular clergy. By alms we rather mean money left to unknown recipients, almost always laymen. The contrast made is between such a form of general benefaction and the specific type of bequest dealt with above. Money left to regular or secular houses is excluded, while that given to hospitals, lazar-houses, alms-houses, etc., is included. So is that left for the general purposes we would lump together as individual charity. Thus through this line of investigation we gain some insight into how the peers viewed and contributed to the social welfare of their social inferiors.

Of the wills leaving an appreciable number of bequests, only about one in three included money for alms. Not only is this proportion strikingly low, but so many otherwise generous wills are excluded from this tally that it is impossible to analyse the eleemosynary practices along lines of familiar or geographical tradition. Though some members of the great families did leave alms, there are too many gaps for us to single out even such groups as the Beauchamps or Montagues for an unbroken pattern. Again, we cannot say that among those who did leave alms, any regular percentage of the bequests went towards this end. The amounts, as well as the end purposes, varied. A minor noble, with only a few bequests, might be quite open-handed, as was James Audley when he left £40 to the poor for their prayers.[3] Others left large sums to religious houses, but were less munificent to the unaffiliated poor. Most who left alms at all did leave respectable quantities.

[3] *TV*, p. 117.

Several different categories of alms can be distinguished. Money given outright at the death of the testator was one category, the subdivisions being into money given to those poor who were present at the time of burial (and who would pray for their benefactor), and to those, absent, who profited through some principle of selection or from the mere phenomenon of the death. As well as the money given the fortunate poor at the funeral, we must remember the not inconsiderable amount of clothing distributed. Money given at anniversaries, chantry services, requiem masses, etc., is also related to funeral alms. There were also bequests of straight cash, handed out to people at a specified future time. Finally, we encounter some bequests made for purposes of general social welfare, and those made to charitable institutions and to their inmates. Most grants within each category varied in both the sums involved and in the details of administration. But the general sameness of the grants was true for the later middle ages as it is of letters of appeal from charitable organizations today. The number of human responses to a small set of social stimuli is limited and not often imaginative.

Bequests were commonly left calling for alms to be distributed to the poor along the route of the funeral procession and at the church of burial. The amounts given away in this fashion were usually spelled out, though sometimes the sum was to cover both burial services and the alms. When the proportions were not specified, the poor probably received the residue after the demands of the church and the officiating clergy were satisfied. Sometimes the number of poor to be aided was stated; this was almost always the case when clothes, rather than cash, were given to those who marched with the body, carrying tapers, torches, and banners. We are reminded here of how public medieval life often was. Simple grants were sometimes found. Roger Beauchamp left £2 to the poor on the day of his burial.[4] Joan Beauchamp stipulated that 1,000 marks were to go towards the cost of her burial, 100 marks for the poor, 'to be dalt penymele'.[5] Margaret Beauchamp asked that twenty-five poor people, at the rate of 1d each, pray for her on the day of her death and again, at the same rate, on the following day.[6] Elizabeth Burgh, customarily generous, left £200 for the poor and for her funeral expenses.[7] Elizabeth

[4] *Test. Karl*, 37, No. 9, p. 87.
[5] Jacob, p. 536.
[6] Dugdale: *Baronage*, I, 250.
[7] *RW*, pp. 23–4.

Clinton asked that £20 be distributed.[8] These are typical of the bequests of straight cash. The payments were probably made by an executor to a cleric of the burial house, and he in turn would superintend the actual distribution. One does not picture the nobles personally putting coin into the hands of their inferiors, except on such ceremonial occasions as Maundy Thursday. They ordinarily used almoners and clerical intermediaries.

We have no idea of how honestly or impartially alms were distributed. The cumulative force of public opinion would have militated against more than the customary amount of embezzlement. Powerful laymen, on the other hand, had but limited personal interest in the actual details of the distribution of their alms: 'They must not, for their soul's health, neglect the duty of dispensing charity: but they need not speculate about the nature of its recipients or its effects upon them.'[9] And yet they would not tolerate too much disregard of their good intentions. The great variable, to the recipients if not to the nobles, concerns the determination of which poor were to get the largesse. The priest on whom this power devolved had a weapon or lever of social control, handed him by a disinterested testator, which he in turn could convert into a petty despotism. In a world where many palms had to be pressed, it was easiest for the benefactor to resign himself to the idea that a certain percentage of alms would remain in the hands of those chosen to distribute them. But a great peer's idea of what constituted an acceptable perquisite may have differed from that of a peasant, hoping for a few pennies in alms to mark the passing of his lord.

As well as straight cash bequests, a few nobles left alms with some interesting stipulations. Thomas Brooke left 4d to each blind or lame person at his funeral, while the whole only received 1d each. All who came to Holydyche manor house after Thomas's funeral services were to get meat and drink.[10] This seems to have been a family tradition, for Thomas's father had posthumously feasted 300 poor, plus an equal number of children, giving 3d to each adult and 1d per juvenile mourner.[11] Thomas Beaufort decreed that the poor carrying torches in his funeral procession were to receive 1d for each year of his life. As he died aged thirty-six, the 3s per man was a considerable boon to

[8] Jacob, p. 267.
[9] Johnstone: *op. cit.*, p. 150.
[10] *Fifty Earliest English Wills*, p. 130.
[11] *Ibid.*, p. 26.

those lucky enough to be chosen.[12] Elizabeth Montague left 25 marks to be spent on 1,000 poor on her burial day, which is 4*d* per person.[13] William Montague ordered 25*s* per day to be distributed to 300 poor men on each day between his death and the arrival of his body at Bisham.[14] Alice Neville turned her back on the alms for prayers, and her 10 marks were for meat and drink.[15] Stephen Scrope left a hierarchical scheme of distribution: ten paupers were to pray at his funeral, at 10*d* each: seven more, at 7*d* each: five at 5*d* per man, and then an additional £2, distributed among all not already provided for.[16]

But this focus on the picturesque should not distract us from the fact that the blander type of provision could be very large indeed: Henry Percy left £20, to be distributed among the poor on the route of the procession, and another £100 to be given out at the funeral itself.[17] John Warenne left £100 for distribution on the day of burial.[18] John Stourton asked for an inexpensive funeral, and 'what is (usually) spent in these uses should be distributed among the poor, though it reach the sum of 20 li'.[19] As early as 1311 William Vavasour left £66 13*s* 4*d* to be distributed, in pennies, on his funeral day.[20] Roger de la Warre, realizing that too little did no real good for the poor, ordered that the £100 he was leaving be distributed 'not by penny dole, but that every person whom my executors may thing fit, shall have half a mark'.[21]

The ubiquitous poor, as well as the curious and the professional beggars, were always willing to supplement their income by forming part of a burial procession. Often they were paid in part by being allowed to keep the new clothes in which they had marched. More ostentatiously than money, clothes were a sign of baronial munificence. Those wearing them formed a sort of servile livery, advertising the generosity of a noble. The sixty poor men who went home in their white gowns from Lord Warenne's funeral were certainly distinguish-

[12] Jacob, p. 356.
[13] *Ibid.*, p. 15.
[14] *TV*, p. 145.
[15] York Consistory Wills, kept at St Anthony's Hall, York.
[16] *TE*, III, 39.
[17] *TE*, I, 57.
[18] *TE*, I, 42.
[19] *Somerset Wills*, p. 145.
[20] *Wills and Inventories*, p. 14.
[21] *TV*, p. 75.

able from their neighbours.[22] When a few men were singled out for new clothes, while many received cash, we are reminded that clothes were welcomed because they were often worth more than the penny or so one stood to gain from the ordinary alms-giving.[23] The gowns gave the anonymous poor an identification with an interest far greater than any they could have hoped to attract on their own. In a society where political power was based largely upon vicarious identification, this may have been another motive on the part of the poor for marching in funeral processions.

Though the usual number of newly-clad torch-bearers was twelve, thirteen, or twenty, even more could be readily found when needed. The Earl of Salisbury wanted twenty-four men, each bearing an 8-pound torch, and each in a black gown with a red hood.[24] John Neville asked that his two dozen torch-bearers be clad in cloaks of russet.[25] Lord Bardolf called for twenty-four men from his estates, to be dressed in black, and twenty-four women, similarly costumed. Each outfit was to cost 8*d*, more than most could expect from a cash distribution.[26] Humphrey Stafford anticipated no problem in finding 100 poor men to march, in white robes with a cross on both breast and back.[27] Funerals probably attracted large crowds, both because of the diversion they offered, and the possible profits. Extra 'walk-ons' could presumably always be found on the spot.[28]

Only a few nobles left money to the poor for prayers at periods long after their deaths. This contrasted with their rich endowment of chantries for masses by specially subsidized clerks. The administrative difficulties of distributing alms, and in instructing ignorant laymen as to their purpose, may have been discouraging. Future prayers were more efficiently said by professionals. John Beauchamp asked that each year, on the anniversary of his death, the prior of the Worcester Dominican house choose forty poor men, each of whom

---

[22] *TV*, p. 154.
[23] Jacob, p. 267.
[24] *TV*, p. 145.
[25] *Wills and Inventories*, p. 41.
[26] Jacob, p. 601.
[27] *TV*, p. 118.
[28] A funeral procession's 'primary object was not charity or the fulfilment of a civic obligation, but to ensure the attendance of as large a crowd as possible at the funeral, and, without too much expense, to place the largest possible number of persons under some obligation to pray for the testator': Douglas Jones: *The Church in Chester, 1300–1540*, Chetham Society, 3rd series, VII (1957), pp. 96–7.

was to receive 1*d* for saying *dirige*, and another 1*d* for a mass.[29] Juliana Clinton left 2*d* to each of 100 poor men on her anniversary.[30] Lord Botreaux said that 2*s* was to be equally distributed among twenty-four poor folk on each Wednesday and Friday for ten years after his death.[31] If carried out fully, this bequest would have cost slightly over £100, a large but hardly extreme amount for alms-cum-prayers.

There was a random, unplanned aspect to the distribution of alms at a funeral or on an anniversary. The nobles rarely sought in their wills to limit or define those who could qualify for their generosity. But some controls might be imposed. One popular method of regulating disbursement was by specifying that the alms were for the testator's own tenants. This emphasizes the existence of bonds other than economic, as well as the sort of proprietorial feelings an aristocrat might feel on his deathbed when casting about for what he could do to help 'his' people. Philip Bardolf left £5 to be divided equally between the poor of Dennington, where he was buried, Brundish, and Tattington, with another £2 14*s* 4*d* cut evenly between the poor of Glenham and Wilburgham.[32] Ralph Basset simply left 16 marks to be distributed among his tenants in Lincoln, 10 marks for those in Leicester.[33] Thomas Beauchamp said that when the alms provided in his will were distributed, the poor at Bordesley, at Worcester, and at Warwick were to be especially remembered.[34] Lady Bergavenny left 200 marks to be parcelled out among her poor tenants, as her executors thought best.[35] This last provision is frequently found. It reflects an acceptance of the testator's helplessness.

The nobles were hardly ignorant of what a windfall a few pence meant to most peasants. John Bigod left £10 to paupers and tenants who *especially* needed it.[36] Favouritism rather than poverty must have been behind Elizabeth Clinton's bequest of 10 marks to her poor tenants at Faversham, while those at Compton Chamberlain received but £2, and those at Claybrook a mere £1.[37] Richard Fitz-

[29] PCC, Logge 13.
[30] Dugdale: *Baronage*, I, 531–2.
[31] *TV*, p. 192.
[32] Jacob, p. 599.
[33] Gibbons, p. 28.
[34] *TV*, p. 79.
[35] Jacob, p. 536.
[36] *TE*, I, 128.
[37] Jacob, p. 267.

Alan left 400 marks for the purchase of land worth £20 per annum, for the poor of 'my' counties of Sussex and Salop.[38] While this was a splendid bequest, it was but a small fraction of all the money distributed in his will, and did not come near the sums lavished upon his favourite churches. Isabella Morley left legacies to her poor tenants in various manors, and to her brethren in the gild of St Andrew, Buxton.[39] William Roos left £200 for division among his poor tenants on several lordships in the north.[40] Other such bequests, if not so large, are readily found. It was a customary form of charity, and may well have been used, in anticipation, to blunt the protests of the rural poor about absentee landlordism. The holidays of the year and the thought of death were apt to make the nobles unwontedly sentimental about those who laboured in the fields.

Money was sometimes left for what we might term 'Christian social work', i.e. charity directed towards specific social reform. The three major forms of such bequests were money to designated types of depressed individuals, money to institutions existing to promote works of charity, and money for public works. Relieving the lot of prisoners was a popular form of public charity.[41] Isabel Morley left money for 'all the prisoners in the Castle and gild hall that lie there, for their fees only, to be discharged by her gift'.[42] Joan Beauchamp wanted the £40 of her bequest to be spent to find and deliver such prisoners as have been 'wel-condicioned', though whether she meant while in jail or in their behaviour we cannot tell.[43] Thomas Montague left £10 to be distributed among the prisoners in London, at the Fleet, Newgate, and Ludgate.[44] Lady Clinton left 6s 8d to each prison in London and Northampton.[45] These last bequests may have been as much for the alleviation of prison conditions as for the release of the incarcerated. Richard Scrope leaves us in no doubt about his intentions: each prisoner at York, Newcastle, Durham,

---

[38] *TV*, p. 95.

[39] Blomefield: *History of Norfolk*, II, 430.

[40] Jacob, p. 24.

[41] Between 1376 and 1531, 25·5 per cent of the wills of Londoners contained bequests for the relief of prisoners. J. A. F. Thomson: 'Clergy and Laity in London, 1376–1531', Oxford D. Phil., 1960, p. 179; H. S. Bennett: *The Pastons and Their England* (Cambridge, 1951), p. 176.

[42] Blomefield: *History of Norfolk*, II, 430.

[43] Jacob, p. 536.

[44] *Ibid.*, p. 392.

[45] *Ibid.*, p. 267.

Carlisle, Richmond, and Appleby was to be given 2s in return for prayers.[46] This was apt to prove expensive, unless northern behaviour was unusually good or law enforcement unusually lax. Thomas Beaufort was generous enough to leave £100 to be distributed among those at Ludgate, Newgate, Fleet, King's Bench, and the Marshalsea prisons.[47] Robert Bardolf left £20 for prisoners, at Newgate, and elsewhere, wherever there was 'necessitas maxime'. This must have applied everywhere. So if relatively few honoured the injunction to succour those in prison, of the scores of noble wills which might have but failed to contain such a provision, those who did take the matter seriously left large bequests for this purpose.

A few other unfortunates were also singled out. Thomas Beaufort left 1s to each of the aged, sick, and debilitated inmates at the London hospitals of St Mary, St Bartholomew, Elsyng hostel, St Thomas, and St Egis.[48] Richard Scrope left 13s 4d to each of his lame or impotent tenants in Richmondshire, and 3s 4d to every blind beggar there.[49] Beatrice Roos acted similarly when she left 6s 8d to seven decrepit members of her household.[50] But such bequests differ in spirit from the £200 which Margaret Courtenay left for distribution among the daughters of knights and gentlemen for marriage portions and for poor scholars at school.[51] Giving money without regard for the identity of the recipient but with concern for his station or condition was in contrast to the practice of tying the bequest to a geographical or seigneurial connection or condition. Joan Beauchamp combined the two purposes by leaving £100 for the marriage of poor maidens living within her lordships.[52] She supplemented the £200 for her poor tenants with £100 specifically designated for the relief of 'bedred men' on her manors.

We have included, as alms, the money left to hospitals and similar institutions when it went for sustenance rather than for original foundation. This qualification removes the major financial help the hospitals did receive. The relevant bequests usually came in the form of straight cash endowments. Sometimes the house itself was the intended recipient, in other instances its inmates were mentioned.

[46] *TE*, I, 274.
[47] Jacob, p. 357.
[48] Jacob, p. 357.
[49] *TE*, I, 274–5.
[50] *TE*, I, 376.
[51] *TV*, p. 127.
[52] Jacob, p. 536.

Robert Hungerford left £2 to the Bethleham poor house, outside Bishopsgate, 6s 8d to the Bradford poor house, and £1 to that at Heytesbury.[53] This was a considerable spread of beneficiaries, considering the slight sums involved. Elizabeth Montague left 26s 8d to each of two west country leper-houses.[54] John Scrope left 1s to each leper-house and poorhouse, called 'Masyndeuxe' in York.[55] Thomas Montague left 300 'scuta Auri' to 'le grant hostel Dieu' at Paris, a house with which he must have become acquainted during his campaigns in France.[56] Without a patron who looked out for the house, it had but small hopes of receiving bequests. The average peer preferred to use alms, distributed immediately before and during his funeral services to those who were present or with whom he already had ties.

Public works did not commend themselves with any frequency. Richard Scrope of Bolton left £40 for work on Wenslaw bridge.[57] His affection for the town and its inhabitants must have been a deep one, for he also left any residue of his estate for the poor there.[58] Bridges were a popular object of endowment, though highways were also mentioned. We know of the adventures that might be encountered on a simple journey,[59] and it is no surprise to learn that goodly sums for public works were needed if the bequest were to make a significant improvement. The sums left for these purposes ranged from the 5 marks Elizabeth Montague left for repairs and emendation of Vennebridge and the £2 for Yverbridge,[60] to the 100 marks Ralph Neville gave for a new bridge at Winston.[61] But, alas, the editor of Neville's will tells us that this project was never carried out. How often this fortune befell the carefully elaborated plans found in the wills cannot be determined, but certainly the non-bridge at Winston was not unique. Lord Hungerford left 5 marks for the repair of a highway called 'le Causway', which his father had built for the soul of 'my mother'.[62] Family tradition carried weight here, and helped bring in money from tradition-oriented nobles.

[53] *Somerset Wills*, p. 187.
[54] Jacob, p. 16.
[55] *TE*, III, 187.
[56] Jacob, p. 392.
[57] *TE*, I, 274.
[58] *Ibid.*, p. 278.
[59] Bennett: *op. cit.*, pp. 128–52.
[60] Jacob, p. 16.
[61] *Wills and Inventories*, p. 73.
[62] *Somerset Wills*, p. 189.

Money was left for the repair and construction of unspecified bridges and roads. Elizabeth Clinton's bequest of 20 marks was to be used when and where it would do the most good: 'to þe amendyng of evel waies and febull brigges þere as myn executours seen moste nede is.'[63] Joan Beauchamp spoke generally of 'makyng and emendyng of feble brugges and foule wayes', and she left £100 toward that end.[64] Robert Ogle simply left £5 for the repair of bridges in Northumberland, particularly on his own lordships.[65] Walter Hungerford built a highway through Stanwick Marsh.[66] More money was forthcoming for the repair of existing bridges than for the construction of new ones. Since the sums left were generous enough to build new projects, it would seem that the countryside may have had an ample number of bridges, and that their upkeep, rather than their augmentation, was called for.

There are several other ways in which the data in the wills can be examined. No pattern emerges for a chronological analysis of the bequests. There is no trend which accounts for the dispersal of either more or less wealth to the church as we go from the early fourteenth century to the late fifteenth. Nor is there any striking pattern of cresting and troughing within the period. Even the mid-fourteenth-century social and demographic crisis, of some significance for alienations in mortmain, does not seem so serious when we look at other forms of philanthropy. From the mid-fourteenth-century we find the same fluctuations between one will and another, between long elaborate lists of bequests and terse references, as we do at the end of the next century. Elizabeth Burgh and William Hastings left as much in alms in Edward III's day as did Richard Scrope in Henry IV's or Thomas Beaufort in Henry VI's, etc. The incidence of wills without many bequests also runs pretty evenly through the period.

To a limited extent the miscellaneous bequests and alms can be arranged by families. But not all members of any family left wills, and so even the best patterns are but approximations. Certain obvious quantitative considerations present themselves. The Nevilles usually left more money to the church, and made more separate bequests, than did the Ogles, the Beauchamps than the Straunges, the Mont-

---

[63] Jacob, p. 267.

[64] *Ibid.*, p. 536.

[65] *Wills and Inventories*, p. 48.

[66] J. L. Kirby: 'The Hungerford Family in the Later Middle Ages', London M.A., 1939, p. 168.

agues than the FitzHughs, etc. But social history must simultaneously seek to fit individual actions into a general framework and yet to remember the separateness of each phenomenon. Elizabeth Clinton, in 1422, left bequests of money all over the Midlands,[67] and so did Robert Bardolf.[68] Yet neither was a person of great prominence, and neither came from a really great family. These people serve to remind us that a minor peer, or his wife, was very wealthy and could, if he or she so chose, scatter money and goods among numerous ecclesiastical houses without impoverishing the family or straining its resources.

Another consideration to be kept in mind is the strong tradition of local patronage. A noble of little national import might well have been of great prominence in his own corner of the realm. His endowments and benefactions there were out of all proportion to the role he played in the Westminster-oriented political scene we are accustomed to accept. This countervailing force helps explain the considerable number of large bequests we find in wills such as those of the nobles from minor families such as Roos and Greystoke.

But after all the qualifications we must reaffirm the basic point that most of the very generous wills are from the greatest families. Some of these merit separate treatment, and the full scope of the bequests can scarcely be touched upon here. Beauchamp, Bohun, FitzAlan, Hastings, Holland, Montague, Mortimer, Neville, Scrope, and Stafford all left numerous wills, replete with generous bequests. But the lesser families of Roos, Willoughby, and de la Zouche can join the select company. Neither the Percys nor the de la Poles, both patrons and benefactors of known prominence, have left testamentary evidence commensurate with their political or philanthropic importance. And the Berkeleys are entitled to a greater share of our attention than they would merit simply on the basis of their wills. So the family is a valid unit for assessing bequests in wills only when other information is brought to bear on our conclusions.

Even within the most philanthropic families, great variation exists between individuals. Different members of a family had different amounts of personal wealth, varying inclinations regarding its ultimate disposition, and different prior commitments. A few specific studies bear this out: the Staffords offer a case in point. Their fortunes rose steadily through the period, but their contributions to the church were barely commensurate with their wealth and import-

[67] Jacob, pp. 266–8.
[68] PCC, Rous 27.

113

ance. The will of Earl Henry, in 1385, only made provision for burial, with some accompanying ceremonies and chantry services.[69] There was no mention of how much cash was to be expended. The stipulations for prayers were modest enough and could have been implemented for well under £50. The will of Elizabeth Stafford, made in 1405, was neither a lengthy nor expansive one, but she did specify that £30 was to be distributed to the poor, and she made separate, if unexceptional provisions for burial and tomb-building.[70] Anne Stafford died in 1439. She left over £120 in cash to the church, about half to her burial place and the rest for a three-chaplain chantry.[71] All of these wills are relatively terse, but they indicate a steady increase in the value, though not in the number of ecclesiastical bequests.

Humphrey Stafford's will, from 1442, brings us into a different realm. The amount of cash he left for the church was greater than anything we have previously encountered in his family. It totals over £180.[72] There are also numerous bequests of personal items, some of considerable value. Almost twenty different churches, regular houses, friaries, and secular chapels shared his largesse, plus the poor at the funeral, and various lepers who were not there. But it is these two characteristics together—more money *and* its wider distribution— which really serve to put this will into the category of major ones. The will of Duke Humphrey Stafford, made in 1460, was rather different. Only a few foundations now shared the bequests, but these now amounted to over £300. Detailed provisions for heavily subsidized prayer services, rather than lists of beneficiaries, occupy most of the will.[73] That of Humphrey, Earl of Devon, written in 1462, barely mentioned bequests; about £10 beyond that spent on the funeral would have sufficed to cover his charities. This document was written by a man with a strong desire to clear his conscience, with good reason, judging from what he tells us. However, he chose to expiate his sins through self-abnegation and prayer, rather than through socially useful philanthropy.[74] The last Stafford will is that of Duchess Anne, who died in 1480.[75] She left £100 to her burial church, and a

[69] *TV*, pp. 118–19.
[70] *TV*, p. 166.
[71] Dugdale: *Baronage*, I, 164.
[72] Jacob, pp. 620–4.
[73] *TV*, p. 296.
[74] *Somerset Wills*, pp. 196–7.
[75] *TV*, pp. 356–7.

bit else for prayers. For a Neville by birth and a duke's widow, this was barely a respectable minimum. What does this brief survey of the Staffords tell us? It mainly shows how difficult it is to plot any tradition even among a group of close relatives over the course of three generations. The peak here came in the middle of the time span. But surely the late fifteenth-century Staffords did not restrain their activities out of a desire for symmetry.

There are five wills of the Scropes of Bolton for the first thirty-one years of the fifteenth century. That of Lord Richard, from 1400, is like that of the first Stafford. Over two dozen institutions and welfare projects are mentioned; the range in bequests was from 3s 4d for each monk in Jervaulx, Coverham, and Eggleston, to several gifts of £40 each.[76] Prisoners, tenants, friars, chaplains of the lord's chapel, and parish priests who sang for his soul were all remembered with cash. A further group of houses and people got vestments, cups, candlesticks, etc. When we enumerate the clergy and the personnel of the houses mentioned, hundreds of folk fell within the web of Richard's generosity. But the next family will, that of Lord Roger, was a small affair. Perhaps the fact that he died only three years after his father helped account for the reduced scale. Roger simply gave £40 to his burial church and a few pounds to the poor.[77]

Stephen Scrope left a will of intermediate length. About £60 was to be distributed among six monasteries, the burial church, the poor, and individual residents of some favoured houses.[78] There was a common practice of leaving money to each inmate of an establishment, and the absence of reference to the number of people involved makes it impossible to guess at the sums being allocated. Richard Scrope tied up much of his estate in a proposed collegiate foundation. His executors were to endow five priests with an income of £10, plus five clerks with an annual income of £3, and three poor servants with £2 each. The size of the necessary investment would have been staggering, and was probably a major reason the college was never established. But we can say that Richard encumbered most of his estate with this single bequest, and only a few other causes were even mentioned, e.g. the local poor, York Minster, and prayers for the mendicants in York and Richmond. The amount of money left was unusually large, the number of recipients unusually small.

[76] *TE*, I, 273–8.
[77] *TE*, I, 329–30.
[78] *TE*, III, 38–40.

Roger's widow Margaret left a will in 1431.[79] She only left about £10 to ecclesiastical beneficiaries, but so adroitly did she distribute this sum that her burial church, its residents, four parish churches, the poor in three separate localities, and the paupers present at her funeral all stood to profit. So it can be seen that the activities of the Scropes of Bolton, one of the more generous of the minor noble families, do not form a distinct picture. This is true both in regard to the number of bequests, their total size and value, and the nature or type of recipient. There were family traditions toward certain houses and possibly toward certain orders, but the ties were never more than guide lines.

We have already considered family traditions of support to the burial church. Is there evidence that ecclesiastical establishments other than the burial house were customarily supported by members of a family? This cannot be completely separated from the other lines of inquiry into family behaviour, for members of a family, living in the same part of the kingdom, would have a natural tendency to support the same institutions without being directly conditioned by family pressures or the location of ancestors' graves. People did not studiously neglect local ecclesiastical establishments. Guy Beauchamp was buried at Bordesley Abbey in 1315:[80] half a century later Earl Thomas bequeathed alms to the poor there.[81] The Dominicans at Worcester, where Margaret Beauchamp was buried in 1477,[82] had been given £20 almost a century earlier by the countess of Warwick.[83] Husband and wife, Richard and Isabella Beauchamp, both remembered Tewkesbury Abbey: he with money, for an obit and a daily mass, she with her wedding gown and other personal possessions.[84]

Elizabeth and Humphrey Bohun both endowed the Dominican house at Chelmsford in their wills. She gave them £20 in 1356, and he gave £10 when he died.[85] They were common benefactors of other friaries also: the London Carmelites (she left 5 marks, he £10), and the London Franciscans (again, she gave 5 marks, he £10). He was

[79] *TE*, IV, 4.
[80] *TV*, p. 54.
[81] *TV*, p. 79.
[82] Dugdale: *Baronage*, I, 250.
[83] *TV*, p. 78.
[84] *TV*, p. 321, 240.
[85] *TV*, p. 60; *RW*, p. 49.

buried in the London Austin Friary, which he had rebuilt, and she left 5 marks to that house. She was buried at Blackfriars, London, and Humphrey gave them £10. This pattern of complementary bequests is interesting, for in this case we have a married couple of generous inclinations. Elizabeth's will contained several hundred pounds of bequests, and Humphrey topped her by several times. But the money left to co-endowed houses represents only a small fraction of all the bequests made. This was true for the Beauchamp activity noted above. The coincidence of endowment between husband and wife never accounted for more than about 20 per cent of the recipients. Married couples with similar interests still went separate ways with 80 per cent or more of their final bequests. No traditions pulled them closer together, and such a scattering of endowments gives us an idea of how competitive the branches of the church were, with few people's money so committed that it was beyond reach of a sufficiently enterprising establishment. Nobody's gifts were tied up in advance.

Elizabeth and Philip Darcy were another couple with partially coincidental bequests. Each patronized the parish church at Knayth: she with her best beast, vestments, and £40 for the fabric, 'pro coopertura laticii borialis cum plumbo', he merely with 16s 8d in cash.[86] Each left money or goods to the nuns at Fosse and to the church at Hennings. Philip bequeathed £1 there, for an alabaster image of St Anne, to be placed at the altar of the Blessed Virgin—a sanguine view of what £1 would buy, even in 1398. Fourteen years after her husband had been buried beside his father at Guisborough, Elizabeth was buried at Hennings, leaving that house vestments, a missal, psalters, 3s 4d to the prior and 2s to each monk, plus £40 for chantry prayers for ten years. The nuns at Fosse also got £40, as against the £2 Philip had left them. In this instance the widow's will was longer and richer than the husband's. This may have been because he predeceased her and she held the bulk of their personal property. Once again, a couple with some common philanthropic interests chose to be buried in separate houses.

These brief family sketches are supported by what we can learn of others—Despenser, FitzAlan, Hungerford, etc. Family traditions of support for churches other than burial houses just barely existed. People felt a qualified attachment to houses in which relatives were buried, or to which some members of the family had already left

[86] *Repingdon*, II, 264; *TV*, p. 146.

money. The feeling, however, was rarely so strong as to command a large part of their bequests. Most individuals who left lengthy wills felt free to embark on a policy of leaving unique or original bequests, i.e. bequests to houses without previous family ties. For all their bonds and their traditionalism, nobles of substance started their list of bequests with the better part of the page blank. They were usually not heavily committed to the institutions supported by their parents or siblings, nor, to a lesser extent by the spouse(s). The exception would be a family with a new foundation to its credit. Then the needs of that house were recognized as being all-important; we have seen that few Montagues neglected Bisham or favoured another house over it, and this is likewise true for the FitzAlans with their Arundel foundations.

It is difficult to make any distinction between the testamentary habits of the sexes. Any such inquiry would also have to take into account which spouse died first, the number, age, and status of surviving children, the intervals between the death of husband and wife, etc. Women were no less generous to the church than were men, and a good share of the longest and most detailed wills are theirs. Women showed perhaps a greater disposition to detail long lists of personal possessions, but many of the common household items may have been considered theirs. They showed solicitude for the poor and, on the basis of the few wills with directions for the distribution of alms, were somewhat more likely than were their husbands to offer money for the relief and release of prisoners, the marriage of poor but virtuous girls, and the support of anchorites and hermits. Women may well have possessed and distributed more books than did men. But much work on this issue must be done before we can speak with any certainty about the wealth and freedom of upper-class women.

Proximity to a peer's residence made a house a strong contender for a bequest. But another consideration is the geographical distribution of the bequests. Over how wide an area were they showered, and what does this indicate, in terms of the testator's lands and sphere of influence? Richard FitzAlan was buried in the Cluniac Priory at Lewes, a foundation long supported by his family.[87] He bestowed bequests upon ecclesiastical foundations at Arundel (supported by income from some of his lands in Sussex), Chichester cathedral, Haughmond Abbey, an old family favourite in the Marches of Wales, Robertsbridge in Sussex, Westminster Abbey, Ely and

[87] *RW*, pp. 120–40.

Canterbury cathedrals, Beverley, etc. A great peer had obligations and expectations to live up to far beyond the geographical centre of his own holdings and residences.

The Hungerfords are quite properly associated with the area around Salisbury. Lord Robert's will called for burial in Salisbury cathedral.[88] His bequests went to the Bonshommes at Edington, Wiltshire and the Austin house at Maiden Bradley. The regular house at Amesbury and various Salisbury friaries received bequests, as did the parish churches of Heytesbury and Teffont Evias, Wiltshire. Farley Hungerford, Somerset, was the main family seat in the fifteenth century, and the parish church there got both cash bequests and a chantry. The poor house at Bradford-on-Tome, Somerset, received 6s 8d. Only the poorhouse outside Bishopsgate, London, drew money away from this localized circle of philanthropic distribution. Walter Hungerford had previously included Bath Abbey among the beneficiaries of his charity.[89]

So two geographical patterns of benefaction emerge, the purely local and the more scattered. Nobody studiously neglected his own area in favour of a distant part of the realm, though many nobles had more than a single home base. The Greystokes left all their bequests to religious foundations in Cumberland and Yorkshire.[90] Peter Mauley's grants went to Doncaster, Lockington in the East Riding, and Denney in Cambridge, this last for the sake of prayers for his mother, who had East Anglian affiliations. The Percys rarely came south of the Yorkshire border, nor did the Scropes venture far from their northern home. But in contrast, a great peer like the Earl of Salisbury might leave bequests to houses in London, Berkshire, Dorset, Hertford, Middlesex, and various places in France, including Caen, See, Falaise, Exmes, and Paris.[91]

A sizeable number of nobles chose burial in London. Did they desert their local institutions for the prestige of the capital? The Bohuns were at home on their Essex estates, and though neither Elizabeth nor Earl Humphrey neglected the institutions there, they did choose London for burial. She left money to the friars of Cambridge, Chelmsford and Exeter, as well as to the church at Rochford.[92]

---

[88] *Somerset Wills*, pp. 186–9.
[89] *TV*, p. 257.
[90] *TE*, I, 117.
[91] Jacob, pp. 390–7.
[92] *TV*, p. 60.

He left money to religious houses in London, Oxford, Cambridge, Essex, Berkshire, and Buckingham.[93] Likewise, Elizabeth Burgh had ties in and near London, and so her burial at the Minoresses' church was hardly a surprise, though her new foundation at Walsingham may have been disappointed.[94] She scattered endowments throughout East Anglia, Bedfordshire, Salisbury, Gloucester, Dorchester, etc. But like the Bohuns, she was a lavish benefactress and that almost guaranteed that her beneficiaries would be geographically scattered. Joan Clinton remembered houses in London and Derbyshire, but the former ones seem to have been her favourites.[95] John Holland, duke of Exeter, displayed hardly any regional favouritism: buried in London, he left bequests to houses in Bedford, Devon, and Hertfordshire.[96]

But conversely London did attract bequests from people whose predominant activities had been in the provinces. An area of special interest *plus* London was a common pattern, subscribed to by peers from many different areas. The Countess of Arundel left £20 to the Friars Preachers in London and £10 to the church of St Mary 'Somerced', while following the family tradition and giving most of her bequests in and around Arundel.[97] William Latimer, buried at Guisborough, showed a strong northern bias, and yet saw no incongruity in leaving £50 to the London Charterhouse, and £10 to the Austin Friars there.[98] The Montagues, as a family, usually stayed close to Bisham, but the Earl of Salisbury left £10 to each of the four mendicant houses in London, and £20 to the Minoresses at the Tower.[99] Elizabeth Neville left £1 3s 8d to these same nuns, though her bequests did not otherwise stray far from the traditional Beauchamp centres of patronage in Warwickshire.[100] Bequests to a London house are found in about 10 to 15 per cent of the wills. Most of the great nobles made such bequests. They were the ones most likely to have spent considerable periods of time in the city. Some had town houses or regular inns, and they were less provincial than their lesser brethren. The cathedral and the mendicant houses

---

[93] *RW*, pp. 44–50.
[94] *Ibid.*, pp. 23–40.
[95] *TV*, pp. 284–6.
[96] *RW*, pp. 282–7.
[97] Jacob, pp. 541–2.
[98] *TV*, pp. 113–15.
[99] Jacob, pp. 390–2.
[100] *TV*, pp. 358–9.

were the establishments profiting most from these 'foreign' benefactions. Parish churches everywhere had to rely more heavily on local patrons, and they could not have expected much from casual residents and visitors to London.

The mendicants, as an order within the church, exceeded any other comparable sub-group in terms of attracting deathbed bequests.[101] Almost every will of substance left something to the friars, though the amounts rarely exceeded £20 (unless it was a burial church or family pet project). The Dominicans and the Franciscans naturally received the lion's share of the bequests, but the Carmelites and the Austin Friars were not completely neglected. The most common bequest was cash: 6s 8d to the friars of Dorchester and the same at Bridgwater, as Lord Stourton's brother requested,[102] or £10 to the Leicester Grey Friars, as Lord Hastings provided.[103] But as well as the scores of cash gifts to specific houses, money was often left to all the friaries within a town, or a county, and sometimes a sum was even left to be divided among the mendicants of a given order within England. A will might contain provision for bequests to three Dominican and three Franciscan houses: £20 to the friaries of the respective orders at Worcester, Shrewsbury, Northampton, Coventry, and Lichfield.[104] Thomas Beaufort left £40 to the Franciscans and £20 to the Dominicans, Carmelites, and the Austins, all to be distributed at his executors' discretion.[105] Elizabeth Bohun left a great sum to the mendicants: £5 to each London friary, besides her bequest to the Dominican house there, where she was buried: £50 to the Friars Preachers at Cambridge, £20 to them at Chelmsford and Exeter, and another 150 marks for other houses, as Friar David de Stirlington 'shall think best for my soul's health'.[106] Lord Botreaux left special bequests to ten different houses, all of £2 each, plus £2 to every mendicant house in Exter.[107] Will after will attests to the posthumous popularity which the friars enjoyed. That money was left to the houses in a certain area, or even to the order itself indicates that the mendicants, and what they still represented to the public, rather than the individual friars and

---

[101] For the late popularity of the mendicants, see E. F. Jacob: *The Fifteenth Century*, pp. 296–8.
[102] *Somerset Wills*, p. 145.
[103] *TV*, p. 371.
[104] *TV*, p. 78.
[105] Jacob, p. 357.
[106] *TV*, p. 60.
[107] *TV*, p. 192.

friaries, were what drew the money. People had confidence that they would use the money as conscientiously and as economically as possible.

Of wills with an appreciable number of bequests, about one in three left money to the friars. Cash was but rarely left to unnamed establishments of other orders, regular or secular, as it was to the friars of a county, etc. If the cumulative totals indicate that non-mendicant regular houses got more money, we must remember the comparative numbers. In 1400 there were over 200 Benedictine houses, alone, with some 2,000 monks, and almost 750 regular houses in all, as against about 185 friaries. The regular orders embraced about 7,000 men and women, compared with 2,000 to 2,500 friars.[108] Furthermore, mendicant houses were rarely the large, sumptuous establishments that their rivals were, and so their needs were correspondingly less. And yet if we except bequests made to burial houses and to those of traditional family ties, we can say that the mendicants received far more, one-fourth to one-third of the regular ecclesiastical bequests.[109] And only they enjoyed popularity as a distinct order of the church, in contrast to the many specific houses to which the nobles had obligations. Cash on hand at the time of death was likely to be left to the friars, through the entire course of the fifteenth century. They kept the respect and affection of the great laymen of the realm, as measured by that most final criterion of all, deathbed legacies.

[108] K & H, pp. 359–64.

[109] This is not unlike data found in other studies. Jones: *op. cit.*, pp. 96–7, 'Thirty-eight of 53 Chester wills made bequests to the Friars, while bequests to the Benedictines were rare.' Thomson's study of London wills shows that 35·6 per cent of the testators left something to mendicants, while only 15·1 per cent left bequests to male regular houses, and only 10·7 per cent to nunneries.

7

⋄⋄⋄

Conclusion

⋄⋄⋄

This investigation is primarily a study of the late medieval nobility. It can, however, be seen in other perspectives: as an inquiry into the role and status of the church and as an investigation of the importance of gift giving and the institutions involved in that process. It is therefore appropriate in this conclusion to say something about each of the different characters in the drama, and to pay particular attention to what philanthropy tells us (or enables us to learn) about their interaction. The separate parts of the picture are not meant to be isolated, and each helped condition and determine the course the others took. Furthermore, social interaction can be negative in the sense that the absence of social interrelations which we might expect to find is a phenomenon no less worthy of notice than their presence.

From this behavioural study of a social group, and an élite group at that, what conclusions can we draw about the English nobility? One of the premises of this work is that the (patriarchal) family offers the best unit around which to organize the data. Does a study of aristocratic gift giving substantiate this? We believe the answer to be 'yes'. Of course, one study does not absolutely prove the case. We scarcely tested other principles of organization against the data as consistently as we used the patrilineal family. Not all the data fitted into neat family patterns. But by and large we can say that the phenomena studied were readily organizable when gathered by families. Furthermore, very little behaviour seemed to defy this principle of organization. When sufficient material could be found indications of family traditions and patterns were not usually hard to identify, though they might be of uneven value. A family's preference for a special ecclesiastical institution or a geographical area was found in many instances. There were some ties toward common family burial sites, though other forces clearly entered in and worked against too much uniformity. There were many indications of traditions of considerable philanthropy within a family, perhaps extended over two or three generations. Of those kin groups which were generously inclined, few so scattered their benefactions or their own remains so as to defy all efforts to make some sense of their behaviour.

On the other hand, while family feeling may have been the strongest single ligature binding together a lot of activity, it had its limitations as a unifier of individualized pursuits. Everyone has some area of freedom, and aristocrats more than most. When they purchased prayers for the dead, the nobles imposed rather narrow definitions upon the functional family—vertical rather than horizontal. Again, where the extant wills allow the point of contrast, husbands and wives only co-endowed a small, albeit significant fraction of each other's beneficiaries. Burial sites united some but almost never all or even most of the members of an aristocratic family. The strongest web of common benefaction was that spun by a family when founding a new house. On those occasions families did concentrate their activities to an extreme degree. In such instances family loyalty might draw members of the kin group together over the course of several generations, as part of a concerted effort to put the new house on a sound footing. But family patterns of unity which transcended more than two immediate generations were rare, and even at this far end of the spectrum not all members of the founding family worked on behalf of the new house. Neither were they all buried in it. Neither did all of their bequests go to that single recipient. Neither did succeeding generations feel indefinitely impelled to take up the challenge. Family tradition could serve to steer a good deal of benefaction in certain directions, but it never became a procrustean bed. As befits voluntary activity, people were always free, to a very large extent, to give or not to give, and to give to whom they chose.

The tie of family was only one form of social bond which affected and influenced the flow of philanthropy. Another was the tie of locality. Strong identification with a certain part of the kingdom, with its inhabitants, institutions, and local traditions was undoubtedly a lubricant which eased the flow of money. Strong local affiliations brought in gifts from families of such varied power and spheres of influence as the Greystokes, Berkeleys, and Scropes, on up to the very greatest noble families, e.g. FitzAlan, Montague, Percy, Neville, and Beauchamp. But like family loyalty, to which it was related, geographical loyalty may have partially governed but it rarely monopolized the disposition of charities. Very few people and very few families gave all their benefactions within just one area, particularly if they ranked among the more munificent donors. Most went farther afield, at least occasionally. There was an obvious desire to be the open-handed lord of the county: this was almost part in fact of the behavioural definition of the English aristocracy when viewed territorially. On the other hand, to spread one's philanthropy around a bit was an easy and practical way of extending one's influence into different areas and of forging ties with élite opinion-makers elsewhere in the realm. The popularity of London for burial sites may be seen as a final try on the part of many provincial aristocrats for such expansionist activity. It was a medieval form of advertising, of public relations: where one displayed oneself was of importance.

Can we speak of the nobility as a social class, acting with any sort of unity or cohesion? The answer is negative in both instances. The variety of behaviour displayed within their ranks in the areas we have investigated was the widest possible—from no recorded philanthropy at all to the most lavish sort of gift giving. If no one ever gave so much as to jeopardize his personal wealth or the family's economic future, at least a tremendous amount of excess wealth went into such forms of conspicuous consumption as new monastic establishments, chantries, tombs, or spectacular public funerals. No single form of activity was practised by everyone or every family, though we see in Appendix I that at least a licence permitting one to make an alienation in mortmain was purchased by almost every family. Presumably most nobles who did leave testamentary bequests left something to some branch or other of mother church, whether it be to the burial house, to an old family favourite, or to a name picked at random from an ecclesiastical gazetteer. The more directed and controlled forms of ecclesiastical benefaction were more expensive, and so they drew fewer people: only about three dozen subsidized new foundations, and only some score endowed their own chantries. Patterns emerge, but no one had to conform, and many did not. It is easier to analyse common behaviour among those who did give than to investigate why their numbers represent but a fraction of all possible donors.

What does this study say about the social cohesion of the parliamentary nobility? Were they a distinct social class, jealously banding together against outsiders? A rather old-fashioned way of evaluating a society, or one of its major sub-groups, is to ask whether the basic characteristics are co-operative or competitive.[1] In so far as this is a valid frame of analysis, the nobility—except within the narrow family units—display the distinct and obvious features of the competitive temperament, set in a social milieu which either actively encouraged such an outlook or accepted it as given and natural. The study of their philanthropy involves us in the social interactions of the nobles. Their competitive impulses and their individualism ran counter to their co-operative tendencies, just as their natural provincialism ran counter to their would-be cosmopolitanism. There were always many checks upon joint endeavours, co-endowments, and the use of common burial sites for non-related peers. Co-operation was always limited, and their individualism, the product of fiercely competitive urges, usually triumphed.

But the desire to compete also manifested itself in a desire to emulate. People asked for tombs like those of other peers who had pre-deceased them and who had attracted posthumous fame through the splendour of their monuments, benefactions, and funerals. The peers all knew each other and it is only to be expected that they kept abreast of each others' gift giving activities. If some chose not to compete at all—and we saw that there were families which left almost no endowments or chantry grants, as there were individuals who left almost no testamentary bequests—others certainly were drawn more deeply into the game because of what their equals had done. In the realm of philanthropy, there was a noted absence of co-operation, except within families. The interaction within the class as a whole was largely competitive—forcing more people to engage in more activity than they might otherwise have done. The sum total of aristocratic benefaction was probably increased because the élite group was so closely interwoven, and yet so unco-operative.

We saw the strong disposition towards including the king and the royal family in the list of people for whom prayers were to be said. This was one of the few instances where politics intruded into our story. The same data revealed a strong disinclination to include the extended family, that very web of relatives underlying so much of the baronial politics of the day, in those prayers. When we examined the support given to *de novo* foundations, we saw that few beyond the

[1] M. Mead, editor: *Cooperation and competition among Primitive Peoples* (New York, 1937, revised 1961). Miss Mead's introduction, pp. 1–19, is particularly useful.

immediate family of the founder became involved in any given project. Regardless of how the peers worked together in politics and war, in marriage-making, in diplomacy, in business ventures, or in drinking and carousing, they pursued aggressively individualistic paths of philanthropy. They were not harmonious, neither were they forced by lack of means into common ventures, as were many men of lesser social status who actually may have had no more regard for each other than did the peers, but who had less freedom of action. The nobles generally kept well out of each others' ecclesiastical endowments. There was little friendly interaction. The picture of the nobility that does emerge is of a group of exclusive, narrowly defined family units. They were conservative in their gift giving. They were not overly given to flights of impulse or to any expansive *bonhomie*, even with those of equal rank and social status.

In terms of the church's popularity with the upper-class laity, as measured by philanthropic activity, we can see both continuity and change. Continuity is marked by what we might call a fairly steady gross aggregate of endowment. In the area of *de novo* foundations the nobles held up a decent standard throughout the period. The major monastic and educational foundations were begun in the fourteenth century, it is true, but there were even more *de novo* fifteenth-century establishments, slightly smaller and poorer though they might have been.

It is easy for us to think of the years before 1307 as the 'good old days', when men entered and left the nobility with ease, and when they gave to the church casually and with an open hand. But the truth about gift giving is more likely to be that there was a natural economic limit to the amount of ecclesiastical endowment that the realm as a whole could afford, let alone any single class within the realm. This limit had been well nigh reached between 1150 and 1350, years of heavy endowment and foundation, corresponding to the two great periods of late medieval spiritual enthusiasm, the age of the Cistercians and that of the mendicants. After 1300 a decline in population, among other factors, began to taper off the growth rate, though there is little reason to think gift giving was among the first institutions to be jettisoned; the contrary may have even been the case for a short while. The first half of the fourteenth century witnessed a steady and significant increase in such acts as alienations in mortmain. But the decline in the number of instances of endowment set in almost immediately after the plague, and it continued throughout the period.

127

If some new aristocrats came along after 1350 and personally worked to create an upward trend, they were more than balanced by both the decline in the total number of families within the peerage and by the decline in the amount of activity per family. Furthermore, the fifteenth-century nobles were every bit as conservative, at least on their deathbeds, as were fourteenth-century ones.

It is impossible to know if the rate of chantry endowment went up or down, owing to the limitations of the extant sources, but the creation of chantries through the course of the fifteenth century was never seriously checked. Nor did later chantry foundations seem to be markedly poorer, or smaller, or intended for a shorter duration than had earlier ones been. Alienations in mortmain did fall off in the fifteenth century, but the fall in quantity was compensated for at least in part by the tendency of each act of alienation to increase in value. There is a general 'tendency to be remarked in the fifteenth century baronage: the absorption of the smaller units by the larger, corresponding perhaps with the economic tendency of the rich to get richer but fewer'.[2] The acquisition of the licences to alienate, when correlated with the increased inherent worth of the alienation, conforms to this view.

Another form of transition within the church, or rather within the realm of popular religious sentiment, is revealed by the shift in concern from regular to secular branches of the ecclesiastical structure. The choice of churches for burial sites was distinctly conservative, i.e. the old monastic and mendicant orders continued to attract many burials and their accompanying endowments. But in most other areas the shift was toward the secular. Chantries came to be set up more and more in parish churches, colleges, or chapels. Alienations in mortmain went in an ever-increasing proportion to secular establishments. In short, while there were internal changes, the church as a whole held its own. Whether this represents a real gain or loss, in view of the economic and demographic trends of the day, is another problem. If there is little impression of unchecked bounty, so there is little of desperation or calculated neglect.

Lastly, what about gift giving or philanthropy as a window into the larger tableau, into the values and *mores* of the society? One of the striking aspects of this study of a ruling élite, seen in the golden age of their power and wealth, is that from it we learn almost nothing

---

[2] Jacob, *op. cit.*, p. 323.

about political configurations. If this is the case, why is it worth doing at all? But this question reflects the politically biased orientation of most of the scholarship, and it can be asked quite differently. Why do the political studies tell us so little about the realms of non-co-operative activity, about the exclusive family networks, etc.? There are more things of importance in medieval society than we can learn just from an investigation of politics. Voluntary behaviour was a vital part of men's lives, just as it was of the social fabric. That the patterns of behaviour found in such a widespread, costly, and popular activity as gift giving fail to correlate with political groupings is a reminder of how politics was but one part of life, and not necessarily the best key to other realms and values. There was little necessary relationship between the rise in political power and status and the propensity to give. Some new families in the aristocracy gave lavishly, others either rose or fell unhindered or unaffected by their lack of benefactions. Some nobles' families fluctuated in their generosity, as personal and local factors moved them. There were many currents in the stream of social life.

To consider the fashion in which the nobles went about practising their good works is to come up against their social conservatism from a different direction. In any situation the gift giver has a tremendous opportunity to exert social control upon the institutions and the *mores* of his world. In modern society, extensive gift giving is directed through both individualized and institutionalized channels. In either fashion it is used to direct and to manipulate the use of human resources and to establish priorities for social welfare and reform, research, education, travel, government policies, the direction of economic growth and development, etc. The social values of the benefactors are protected by their generosity, and to some extent the values are imposed or grafted onto their beneficiaries. The social status of the givers is enhanced by their seemingly gratuitous attempt to rectify social ills. The philanthropists themselves, realizing that conspicuous charitable activity is a safety valve for discontent, also like to believe that they are alleviating any social guilt they (or their ancestors) incurred while gathering their inequitable share of the wealth. The rest of society usually is willing to accept their activities and motives at face value, and only the radical critic today attacks gift giving as being part of a design to perpetuate social ills rather than to rectify them.

These general considerations are applicable to medieval society, as they are to modern. At first glance the aims of medieval gift giving and charity may seem too different to admit of comparison. Medieval charity was primarily aimed at the spiritual welfare of the donor, rather than at improving the worldly condition of the recipient. Philanthropy directed toward social reform was singularly absent from the late medieval world, both in theory and in practice. Whatever the church did to ameliorate the lot of the unfortunates of this world, they took care to be the administering intermediary between any lay gifts received for that end and the ultimate disposal of those funds.

But this difference between the medieval and modern situation is more apparent than real. In either instance the main social function of the charity is to apply social control by the benefactor upon the beneficiaries, both the intermediate and the ultimate ones. The creation of networks of reciprocal relationships, between nobles and the church, nobles and the poor, the church and the poor, etc., was correctly seen at the time as the logical and proper end of the gift giving. That there were spiritual as well as social and economic purposes being served by the gift giving does not alter this reality, though it does mean that to a very large extent the networks of interdependence were spiritual rather than political or economic. The documents we have examined certainly indicate that the medieval aristocracy gave its gifts with care, deliberation, and self-consciousness. The nobles were willing to pay, sometimes handsomely, for the privilege of bestowing gifts upon the church. Many of them gave generously. But without exception, they gave in keeping with known social traditions and patterns. They might have attached complicated conditions to their grants. They might have added long and revealing preambles to their grants, telling us about themselves, their money, and their view of their place in the process. They must have been aware of the manipulative value of their gifts, in both the economic and the moral sphere.

But they did not seek to take control. Conservatism is the keynote of their charity when we view it in terms of its potential for social control. A study of gift giving reveals the deep conservatism of the aristocracy, whether measured by the ways in which they gave, the amounts they gave, or the stipulated ends for which they gave. If there was a class in medieval society which might have worked to alter the policy of ecclesiastical interposition between giver and recipient, it was the aristocracy. But they never did so. They were neither moved in this direction by religious conviction nor by any grasp of class consciousness, nor by any thirst—collective or individual—for economic or moral aggrandizement. In so far as their charities had ecclesiastical recipients as the ultimate beneficiaries, they exerted little leverage beyond asking for the standard return, i.e. prayers (though these were usually endowed at a very fair rate). They did not try to use their money for bold or unorthodox ventures. They sought neither to cause social change nor to influence others in a direct way. The concept of the gift as a powerful lever for social change or control was never developed in their hands. They gave their money, but they gave in the expected ways, for traditional ends.

The picture of gift giving we have seen hardly represents a shining example of enlightened self-interest. An aristocracy which exhibits no inclination to convert its considerable economic power and contributions into effective social control is an aristocracy likely to find its exalted position becoming increasingly hard to maintain. The reluctance of the nobles to manipulate others, both in their actions and in their values, is an indication of their limited comprehension of their class interest. High social status is constantly under attack, both from social rivals and from the forces of natural attrition. Gift giving is the sort of activity easily turned to advantage, particularly since the nobles were already paying the piper rather handsomely. They could have simply redirected the process; there was no need to create a new bureaucracy or to dig new channels.

For an élite group to be so obtuse in regard to the manipulative value of a critical form of action, in the face of pressures from new capital, from competing classes, from urbanized political power, and eventually from an aggressive monarchy was ultimately to help close the social gap between the nobility and the rest of lay society. Without legal barriers to separate the nobility—and there were none in England—class-consciousness was sorely needed to preserve the élite status. Class-consciousness did exist in politics, but hardly at all, it would seem, in the realm of voluntary social action. The tragedy, from the view of the aristocracy, was that in these latter realms men often have more freedom of action and more scope for initiative, than in the arena of public life.

The English nobility, in so far as their gift giving offers an insight into their social identification or social self-consciousness, must be given low marks. They failed to utilize their extensive gift giving for purposes of social control and personal aggrandizement. They failed to assert themselves in the direct distribution of their gifts. They neither questioned the church's set of values nor did they make it work explicitly and visibly for their purposes (which were generally left undefined). They fed a system which needed their money but which showed little inclination to preserve their status, as it did the king's. Through their gift giving they were doing little to widen the gap between themselves and others; a gap which other forces regularly worked to narrow. They allowed the distinction between noble and commoner to be seen as simply a quantitative one. The rich— whether noble or not—gave to the church, but there was no differentiation between the givers by rank. No hereditary aristocracy can afford to stand aloof in this fashion.

But we must not conclude with the impression that the church was deliberately fleecing the nobles for its own purposes. A church is hardly in the best health when it is attracting a diminishing share of its wealth from the upper class. Such an ecclesiastical establishment has failed to maintain contact with its natural ally, perhaps because it is not offering enough in return. Ecclesiastical self-interest does not seem to have been much better formulated than was aristocratic self-interest. Upholding a privileged position—be it secular or spiritual, economic or social—takes as much luck, talent, and imagination as does winning that position in the first place.

Both the economic and moral consequences of gift giving serve to make it an important social phenomenon, particularly in a society with a venerated institutional outlet for philanthropy. The religious system, the social welfare system, the education system and the pool of surplus manpower were all tied into the system of gift giving and distribution. And yet it is impossible to say that late medieval philanthropy was a basic causal factor in social change. W. K. Jordan chose 'A Study of the Changing Patterns of English Social Aspiration' as the subtitle for his *Philanthropy in England*.[3] This would be inadequate and inappropriate for the fourteenth and fifteenth centuries. Social aspirations remained much the same, at least within the upper classes throughout these years, and really significant social change was more conspicuous by its absence within the upper classes than by its presence. Perhaps the hereditary aristocracy is not the place to seek for signs of change, though it might well seem the place to seek indications of class-consciousness and of the knowledge of how status is converted to power and control. But we still know very little about anything other than the political and economic affairs of

[3] W. K. Jordan: *Philanthropy in England, 1480–1660: A Study of the Changing Patterns of English Social Aspiration* (London, 1959).

the late medieval aristocracy. When we have yet to establish a *status quo*, it is premature to worry overmuch about change.

A recent study of gift giving in ancient Greece and Rome shows two tendencies which are also borne out by our medieval data.[4] One was the inclination of donors to give in such a way as to rebound to their own credit without having to worry very much about the recipients of the charity who were suffering from poverty, disease, hunger, and chronic hardship. The other was the policy of using the state (the *polis*) or a guild or fraternity or perhaps a religious society as an intermediary between the benefactor and those who stood in need of the benefactions, and of thereby allowing another party to manipulate the recipients. Thus we see that the shortcomings of the English nobility, both in terms of charitable sensitivity and of class interest, were not peculiar to their day or status. Through the ages donors have been only too willing to turn over the administrative details of their gift giving to intermediaries. The surrender of social leverage is the inevitable and proper consequence of this policy. The nobility did little to enhance their own status or power as a group, for all their charity. They did little to further the secularization of society which was so prominent a feature of post-Reformation gift giving.[5] They bought their prayers and they were mostly content to dream of the splendid monuments which would one day stand over their mortal remains. Men of this sort may topple kings but they do not change the values or social institutions of their world.

[4] A. R. Hands: *Charities and Social Aid in Greece and Rome* (Ithaca, 1968). The statement on p. 88 is representative of the general assessment of charity and social concern: 'In this giving, however, we may safely generalize that the poorest class of society was never singled out for specially favourable treatment.'

[5] R. M. Kingdon, 'Social Welfare in Calvin's Geneva', *American Historical Review*, February, 1971, pp. 50–69. 'Two essential principles characterized almost all of these reforms; laicization and rationalization.' We may say equally well that these were hardly to be found in pre-Reformation England.

Appendix I

Alienations in mortmain

Previous chapters have dealt with the substance of gift giving. This Appendix is separated from the bulk of the study because it focuses on a legal form or method of philanthropy more than upon the bequests themselves. The nobles who purchased licences to alienate property in mortmain to the church are here lumped together because they conformed to a particular legal prerequisite or procedure. The actual gifts which the licences permitted them to make are not necessarily related to each other in any way except through the use of this one form of legal action. Consequently we look here at an instrument of government as well as the desired end result, benefaction, and we set this chapter apart from the rest of the study, where the gift itself was of primary importance.

Edward I promulgated the Statute of Mortmain in 1279.[1] It forbade the alienation of real property to the church, whether held in chief or not. There is no indication in the statute that the crown actually contemplated the control of alienation, rather than its cessation.[2] In any event control, rather than cessation, was achieved, and this took the form of licensing each permitted act of mortmain (and of recording the licence in the patent rolls of Chancery). Through the licences we can follow the stream of alienations made by the

---

[1] F. Pollock and F. W. Maitland: *op. cit.*, I, 240–51, 333–4, and T. F. T. Plucknett: *The Legislation of Edward I* (Oxford, 1949), pp. 94–102, 109. The problem of alienations in mortmain prior to 1279 is dealt with in Charles Gross, 'Mortmain in Medieval Boroughs', *American Historical Review*, XII (1907), pp. 733–42. Also, K. L. Wood-Legh: *Church Life under Edward III* (Cambridge, 1934), pp. 60–88, for specific case studies and a general survey, and H. M. Chew, 'Mortmain in Medieval London', *English Historical Review*, LX (1945), pp. 1–15.

[2] T. F. T. Plucknett: *Statutes and Their Interpretation in the First Half of the 14th Century* (Cambridge, 1922), p. 144.

nobles. While the letters patent do not tell all we might wish to know about the alienations, in them we have a complete record of the instances of use of one form of philanthropy. Conclusions based on a study of the licences are less impressionistic and fragmentary than those based on other forms of records. At the same time we must bear in mind that the licences were issued by the king for his own purposes, and that there are some aspects of benefaction and endowments on which they shed almost no light.

The licences were readily obtained. They were issued to the nobility in some profusion throughout the fourteenth century and in lesser, though substantial numbers, during the fifteenth century. They are the most commonly employed instrument of endowment and through them almost all the noble families of the land bestowed property upon some branch of the church. Real property of various sorts and of widely ranging values was given to foundations in most of the counties of England and to a few counties in Wales. Old establishments were enriched, and many new ones were founded and first endowed through these licences. A systematic study of the licences, and of the alienations thereby permitted tells us much about many different aspects of philanthropy. But we must remember that what is being examined are the *instances* of benefaction, rather than the benefaction *per se*. How often the noble families gave, to whom, and where, and what they gave are illuminated. Analysis of the alienations sheds some incidental light on the quixotic practices of a government which had promulgated a Statute of Mortmain and which then chose to enforce it in a way not even mentioned in the statute.

For the years between 1307 and 1485 the Calendars of the Patent Rolls record some 450 licences to alienate issued to the nobles. The data from these licences is broken down in Table 8. For easy analysis we have broken our two-century span into seven periods, corresponding to moments of political transition (with Edward III's reign also being cut at 1348, the year in which the plague first struck England).

The data in the table seemingly verify two generally accepted views. Firstly, that there was a definite decline in lay support of the church in the fifteenth century in terms of the number of licences issued: only 21 per cent of all the licensed alienations were made after 1399 (93 alienations of a total of 446). Furthermore, within our seven periods, there were forty-two separate years in which no licences were issued at all to the nobles. No such years can be found in the first two periods. Then the number of blank years within each respective period was one, four, nine, sixteen, and twelve. So of the 86 years between 1399 and 1485, 37 passed without any nobleman even receiving a licence to alienate; there were periods of from two to seven consecutive years in the century when no licences were issued to the peers. The mean number of per-annum licences in the fifteenth century was but 1·08, as against a fourteenth-century mean of 3·84, and an over-all mean of 2·52.

TABLE 8   Percentage of licences permitting alienations, by years and recipients

Years	% to regulars	% to nuns	% to friars*	% to seculars	% to misc.	% Total	Total licences	Mean number of licences per year
1307–27	54	4	17	21	4	100	48	2·3
1327–48	48	2	9	33	8	100	169	7·7
1348–77	43	8	10	33	6	100	84	2·9
1377–99	46	0	12	35	8	101†	52	2·4
1399–1422	52	0	0	44	4	100	23	1·0
1422–60	26	0	2	67	4	99†	49	1·3
1460–85	19	0	5	71	5	100	21	0·8

* These percentages include licences granted to houses of Franciscan nuns.
† Totals in this column do not always equal 100 per cent because of rounding error.

The second point illustrated by Table 8 is the progressive decline in lay support for regular branches of the church. Conversely, secular ecclesiastical establishments became increasingly popular in the fifteenth century, at the expense of their regular rivals: of the fourteenth-century licences only 32·3 per cent had gone to secular institutions (112 of 329), while the fifteenth-century figure, based as it was on many fewer licences, was 62·3 per cent (58 of 89). There was some resurgence on the part of male regular houses in the reigns of Henry IV and Henry V. However, the total neglect of nunneries in the fifteenth century, and the greatly diminished support given to the friars more than balanced this upswing—a rise from 46 per cent of the licences in Richard II's time to 52 per cent between 1399 and 1422. Support for the seculars had increased gradually through the fourteenth century, going from 21 per cent of the licences to 35 per cent, but it began going up dramatically after 1399, eventually reaching the figure of 71 per cent.

The golden age of alienation was between the accession of Edward III and the outbreak of the plague. Over three times as many licences were issued then as in Edward II's reign, and over twice as many as in the period 1349 to 1377. But if the plague brought the period of heavy endowment (as expressed by licences to alienate) at an end, the decline in the immediate generation after 1348 was still at an annual level above that of any other period. And in terms of recipients, no new trends seem to have set in immediately after the greatest social catastrophe since the barbarian invasion. The major trends—a steady decline in the percentage of regular recipients, a steady increase in the percentage of secular ones—ran straight through the entire period.[3]

There are several qualifying factors to consider in assessing the decline in the number of fifteenth-century licences. Most fourteenth-century ones had simply permitted the alienation of a specific bit of real property (or the cash rent from such property). In the fifteenth century there was a higher incidence of licences for the actual foundation of the recipient institution, and for its original endowment. There was also an increase in the number of 'general' licences, i.e. licences which enabled the recipient to alienate property as yet undesignated, to be chosen at some future point and to be specifically approved in a future licence.[4] These two types of licence, the founding and the general, made up approximately 30 per cent of the fifteenth-century licences (33 of 93) as against but 8 per cent of the fourteenth-century licences (29 of 353). This also means that, per licence, the value of alienated property named on fifteenth-century licences was likely to be greater than it had been in the fourteenth-century. Fewer nobles sought licences to alienate those small and relatively valueless bits of property which had been named on many of the fourteenth-century licences.

A table does not tell the entire story. Each peer saw himself as a free agent, and our efforts to fit him into what we consider to be a pattern or category should not obscure the basic individuality of each source. In some ways the nobles, standing so near the pinnacle

---

[3] D. Knowles: *The Religious Orders in England* (Cambridge, 1955), II, 3–13, on the importance in religious history of the watershed of 1348–9.

[4] A general licence runs thus: 'License for John de Neville of Raby to alienate in mortmain the advowson . . . to any ecclesiastic, secular or religious, and for them to appropriate the same.' *CPR 1377–81*, p. 235.

of the social structure, were relatively free to pursue whatever course of action they chose. But in other respects they stood in the light of public attention, and they were particularly fettered by tradition and by pressures to compete and to emulate. We are dealing here with so many instances of alienation that some general patterns and trends can be identified. The unusual items catch our interest, and the ordinary ones provide the framework of the inquiry.

The items most commonly alienated were arable land, the rents from farmed property, and the advowsons of parish churches. This is true through the entire period. Alienated property ranged from a small plot or tenement to aggregates of many manors and hundreds of acres. The friars usually received mere plots, either for the creation of new houses or, more frequently, for the enlargement of already existing ones. The plot in Bristol, 100 feet square, given by Simon Montague to the Austin Friary there, was typical of these alienations, both in its size and its proximity to the already standing house.[5] These small but conveniently located pieces of land must have been welcomed by the urbanized mendicants: witness the plot, 8 by 3½ perches in Orford, adjacent to the old Austin house, granted by John Engaine,[6] or the two acres for enlargement of their premises, acquired by the Lichfield Franciscans from Ralph Basset of Drayton.[7] The grant of a well, water from which was borne via an underground conduit, must have been greatly appreciated by the Friars Minor of Lynn.[8] These petty alienations would not have gone far to satisfy the needs of larger institutions, and most nobles had to be willing to part with more property when they made their endowments.

Land was the most common grant. Sometimes it was near the recipient's domain. In other instances it was far afield, and the collection of revenues was simply passed from the hands of one set of officials, acting for an absentee landlord, to those of another set similarly engaged. The grant might be 60 acres of wood, or 11 tofts and 11½ bovates, with the added reversion of 3 tofts and 3½ bovates, or 100 acres of pasture, or perhaps an entire manor.[9] The pieces of land were eccentric in both size and value. Small alienations and large were made both early and late in the period, in all regions of

[5] *CPR 1307–13*, p. 596.
[6] *CPR 1313–17*, p. 82.
[7] *CPR 1327–30*, p. 465.
[8] *CPR 1313–17*, p. 128.
[9] *CPR 1317–21*, p. 559, *CPR 1350–54*, p. 137, and p. 396, respectively.

England, by families great and small, old and new. Cash rents were given away almost as frequently as was land. The exact amount of rent is usually, though not invariably, specified. In many cases the licence to alienate covered both land and rent, lumped together in such a way as to indicate that they were hardly distinct in the benefactor's own mind, or in his manorial accounts. Time after time grants such as that of Thomas Wake are found: 45 acres of arable, 19 of meadow, and 25s 6d in rent.[10] A more elaborate combination is also encountered: the manor of Catford by Lewisham, a messuage, a mill, 300 acres of land, 20 of meadow, 60 of pasture, 40 of wood, plus an additional 26s 8d in rent, all on the same licence.[11]

Even apart from the great alienations for foundation purposes numerous grants of substance were made. A chantry priest was expected to live on an income ranging from £4 to 10 marks: any donation which returned more than this can be viewed as a not insignificant grant. If Robert de Vere's manor of Manbridge, Hampshire, was truly worth the 24 marks at which he assessed it, he was being more than generous in alienating it to the house at Netley.[12] The manor of Caldecot was only worth £10, but Ralph Hastings was still being open-handed when he granted it to St Mary chapel, Nosely.[13] Henry Percy released all but 1d of the £20 which Sawley Abbey had paid annually to Henry's family.[14] But if these grants were substantial, they were not princely. Few really gigantic benefactions and foundation endowments were made through licences to alienate.

Advowsons of churches were held by common law to be the private possession of the patron, and they were alienated in profusion.[15] The later middle ages saw an increasing amount of 'the tithes of benefices passing into the hands of corporate bodies through the

---

[10] CPR 1330–34, p. 67.
[11] CPR 1338–40, pp. 103–4.
[12] CPR 1327–30, p. 262.
[13] CPR 1367–70, p. 246.
[14] CPR 1391–96, p. 69.
[15] Pollock and Maitland: op. cit., II, 136–40; E. Jenks: A Short History of English Law (London, 1920), pp. 93–4; Felix Makower: Constitutional History of the Church of England (London, 1895), pp. 295–6; H. Maynard-Smith: Pre-Reformation England (London, 1938), pp. 39–40. The possession of an advowson was not supposed to be a source of profit, though it usually was: R. H. Snape: English Monastic Finances in the Later Middle Ages (Cambridge, 1926), p. 77. It has been noted that at the Reformation 63 per cent of all parishes in York diocese were appropriated (392 of 622), though this probably was above the national average: A. H. Thompson: The English Clergy (Oxford, 1947), p. 115.

practice of appropriations', and the nobles come in for their share of credit or blame on this account.[16] Some licences quote the value of the advowson being alienated—£12, £20, etc.[17] John Charleton alienated the advowson of the church at Pontesbury to Haughmond Abbey, but since the advowson was divided into three portions, the Abbey was only to realize its new possession as each portion fell vacant.[18] The system whereby the parishioners received vicarious spiritual care from the rector assured that, though the church was passed on to another patron, the flock in theory would still be looked after by a vicar. There may have been no greater neglect of pastoral duties now than when the lay lord had exercised direct patronage, though the temptation to neglect must have been enhanced each time the living changed hands. Sometimes care of the flock was specified as a condition of alienation and appropriation. In these few instances the people of the parish may have profited spiritually by the alienation. But concrete evidence is lacking, and this conjecture is a sanguine one.[19]

Though the value of the property alienated could be quite considerable, most alienations were worth under £5. The rents given, either alone or in conjunction with land, usually ran from a few shillings to several pounds. The advowson of a parish church and a small plot of land in that village, perhaps adjacent to the churchyard, was considered a reasonable alienation, judging from the frequency with which it was made. When 100 acres of pasture might only be valued at 3s 4d, often a large bit of property represented but a small financial sacrifice.[20] Gilbert Talbot granted 3 messuages of land, 64 acres, 2 of meadow, 11 of pasture, 14½ of wood, and 23s 10d of rent—the messuages and the land only having clear yearly value of 12s.[21] Quite a bit of acreage was sometimes needed before the alienated property could support a priest or subsidize some building project.

Occasionally a licence to alienate permitted the transfer of more unusual items. Property was still graphically described as pasture for two horses, four oxen, and 200 sheep, or a common yearly pasture for sixty oxen.[22] Again, odd payments and perquisites were found among

[16] E. F. Jacob: *The Fifteenth Century* (Oxford, 1961), p. 278.
[17] *CPR 1348–50*, p. 20, and *CPR 1370–74*, p. 454.
[18] *CPR 1313–17*, p. 618.
[19] Jacob: *op. cit.*, p. 279, for the deterioration of vicarages.
[20] *CPR 1327–30*, p. 137.
[21] *CPR 1334–38*, p. 270.
[22] *CPR 1327–30*, p. 21, and *CPR 1401–5*, p. 495.

the more orthodox lots. John Cobham, *inter alia*, alienated an annual rent of 21 quarters of wheat and 3 bushels of barley.[23] Late medieval rents had not completely lost all vestiges of an earlier day, and we still discover a rent of a capon, two cocks, three hens, and eight autumnal works, a pound of pepper, an annual payment of a rose, or 2 pounds of cumin, fourteen autumnal works, and a carriage.[24] Though the nobles mostly possessed and alienated rural lands and possessions, a few tenements in London were granted. William de la Pole granted a tenement, held of the king in burgage tenure, to the Corpus Christi Chapel of St Lawrence Pulteney parish church in 1447.[25] In Richard II's reign Richard FitzAlan alienated a tenement in the parish of St Swithin's, Candlewick Street, to Tortington convent.[26]

Why did men alienate their valuable property to the dead hand of the church? For the most part, of course, in return for the good offices and prayers of the beneficiaries. Because the exchange of temporal possessions for spiritual returns was such an accepted part of the social web, no one was reticent about stipulating that reciprocal services were required. Slightly over one-third of all the licences explicitly called for prayers.[27] Table 9 shows the proportion of the licences with such a specific demand. The obligation to pray was never fastened on to less than a quarter of the licences in any given period.

TABLE 9 Licences to alienate stipulating prayers in return

Years	Total licences	% with stipulation of prayers
1307–27	48	27
1327–48	169	36
1348–77	84	37
1377–99	52	23
1399–1422	23	26
1422–60	49	46
1460–85	21	48

[23] *CPR 1361–64*, p. 265.
[24] *CPR 1367–70*, p. 88, *CPR 1338–40*, p. 89, *CPR 1327–30*, p. 304, and *CPR 1452–61*, pp. 478–9.
[25] *CPR 1446–52*, pp. 122–3.
[26] *CPR 1377–81*, p. 351.
[27] Wood-Legh: *op. cit.*, pp. 73–4: 'Nearly two-thirds of the mortmain licences that concern the monasteries sanctioned grants which appear to have imposed no specific obligations on the recipient.'

In the mid-fourteenth century, 36 per cent (between 1327 and 1349) and 37 per cent (between 1349 and 1377) of the licences enjoined this obligation. After 1422 almost half of the licences called for prayers. This is in keeping with the general distinction noted above between fourteenth- and fifteenth-century licences; fewer alienations in the latter century, but a higher percentage of those made were now major ones, with more indication of interest in and direction of the use of the endowment. It is noteworthy that no more than 35 per cent of all the licences, through the entire period, explicitly mentioned prayers. We might have expected a higher proportion. But once again we must remember the limited purpose of the licences. Government records were only incidentally the place where men recorded their fears for their eternal souls.[28] We shall see below strong evidence of an interest on the part of many benefactors in helping souls, their own and others, pass through the rigours of purgatory.

Apart from those licences which called for prayers, only a few indicated some continuing concern with the use to which alienated property would be put. Some asserted that the property was for the maintenance and sustenance of the clerical recipients: 'in augmentation of their pittance'.[29] Instructions of greater interest are those where the grantor specified that the parishioners of the alienated advowson were not to suffer spiritual or economic loss. The Countess of Kent alienated an advowson to Bourne Abbey, and made it conditional upon the vicarage being adequately endowed, and a 'competent sum of money from the fruits of the church (being) distributed yearly among the poor parishioners'.[30] The Nevilles made a similar provision.[31] But the grantor's directions were not always of this sort. Wormegay Priory received the appropriation of a Norfolk advowson and gained the right to serve it with one of their own canons or other equitable chaplain, without the necessity of endowing a

[28] The nobles seem to have been confident that their conditions would be met. It is not unusual to find a licence like that issued to James Audley in 1359, where he enumerated the items in his benefaction, and in return for the grant asked the monks of Darley to 'celebrate divine service in the abbey according to an ordinance to be made': *CPR 1358–61*, p. 289.

[29] *CPR 1313–17*, p. 30. Sometimes a house was singled out for benefaction because its fortunes were known to be at low ebb: 'in consideration of the losses sustained by . . . frequent attacks of the Scots': *CPR 1334–38*, p. 36; or 'whose possessions have been in great part burned by the Welsh rebels so that divine service and other charges and works of piety cannot be maintained there according to the ordinance of foundation': *CPR 1405–8*, p. 192.

[30] *CPR 1408–13*, p. 387.

[31] *CPR 1408–13*, pp. 426–7; *CPR 1441–46*, p. 185; *CPR 1467–77*, p. 410.

vicar.[32] Chantries were endowed under conditional grants, with the alienated property being revocable if the grantor or his heirs were dissatisfied. The de la Poles, in alienating land to the mayor and commonalty of Thetford for a municipal chantry of two chaplains, retained the 'right to distrain should any defect arise hereafter in finding such chaplains: provided that the same can be done without prejudice to the king or others'.[33]

Prayers for the souls of the benefactors and others were the only reciprocal service mentioned on any appreciable number of licences. About two-thirds of the licences just present bald statements of what was alienated. Alienations to the friars are an exception of sorts, for eighteen of the twenty-eight licences made to male mendicant houses in the fourteenth century specified that the small plot of land was to go for the building or the enlargement of the friary. Beyond this, few licences carried anything we can interpret as instructions or even a close awareness of the use to which the new property would be put. Most grants merely helped swell the house's general revenues. Only a few licences specified enlargement: a messuage in Huntingdon went towards the parsonage's growth,[34] and four acres of land (exchanged for 21s of rent in Bristol) for the Hospital of St John of Jerusalem.[35]

Not many licences trailed off into generalities about 'other works of piety'. A few stipulated that poor men were to be fed, either daily or perhaps on the anniversary of the death of the grantor's wife.[36] One fifteenth-century licence endowed a hermit, among whose duties was the practical burden of highway repair.[37] Two fourteenth-century licences were unusual in that they alienated advowsons in order to help maintain female relatives of the donor in nunneries.[38] The general lack of direction and instruction, reflected in most licences, is probably misleading. It was not that benefactors were indifferent as to the disposition of their property, but rather that licences are a poor key to this concern.

In her survey of alienation in mortmain Miss Wood-Legh observes that the fines paid for the licences bore no fixed relation to the value

[32] *CPR 1413–16*, p. 349.
[33] *CPR 1441–46*, p. 135.
[34] *CPR 1321–24*, p. 298.
[35] *CPR 1343–45*, p. 305.
[36] *CPR 1345–48*, pp. 141, 169.
[37] *CPR 1446–52*, pp. 180–1.
[38] *CPR 1361–64*, pp. 111, 234. This was a rare practice: Wood-Legh: *op. cit.*, pp. 74–5.

of the property being alienated. There was a whimsical nature to the fees or fines—some licences being issued free, others bringing in a considerable amount of cash.[39] An examination of these fees might provide an indication of whether a governmental policy behind the granting of the licences emerges, as well as showing how willing the nobles were to pay for the freedom to make alienations, whereas personal possessions left in wills or given in one's lifetime needed no comparable royal approval. Of the 450 licences under consideration here, 131 were issued upon receipt of a fee or a fine (i.e. a payment from the beneficiary for having prematurely taken possession of the alienated property). There were very few fines, paid by the recipient, in comparison to the fees paid by the donor. In the reigns of Edward II and Edward III 61 licences were paid for, in Richard II's time 23, in Henry IV's 10, none in the reign of Henry V, 25 in Henry VI's time, and 12 under the two Yorkist kings. Thus about half the fees were assessed before the death of Edward III, about half between 1377 and 1485. But two-thirds of all the licences (301 of 446) were issued before 1377. Thus we discover that in the last 108 years the proportion of licences issued upon payment of fee or fine was a good bit higher than it had been between 1307 and 1377. Before 1377 only 23 per cent of the licences were paid for, as against 58 per cent of those issued after 1377. After 1377, when fewer licences were being granted, there was a smaller proportion of the simple grants and a higher one of licences to found or to endow heavily. After 1377 the nobles were paying more money, more frequently, for their licences, but they were making more valuable (if fewer) alienations. Of course, noting this phenomenon does not explain it.

Before 1377 the fees were usually under £10, though there are numerous exceptions. Sawley Abbey paid a fine of 80 marks for appropriating a Yorkshire advowson granted by Henry Percy.[40] Alan de Zouche paid £40 to alienate an acre of land and the advowson of the parish church of North Moulton, Devon.[41] Henry Vavasour paid 20 marks in 1331 to alienate an advowson,[42] and Robert Holland's widow paid 24 marks to alienate a rent of 14 marks.[43] John Grey of Rotherfeld paid 100 marks to alienate the advowson of Oxborough, Norfolk, and yet there is nothing special about this

[39] *Ibid.*, pp. 61–4.
[40] *CPR 1313–17*, p. 11.
[41] *Ibid.*, p. 30.
[42] *CPR 1330–34*, p. 103.
[43] *CPR 1334–38*, p. 33.

alienation except the unusually heavy fee.[44] But against these fees are innumerable ones of £5, 1 mark, ½ mark, £1, 5 marks, 40s, etc. The average nobleman, when forced to pay for his licence, was not set a fee which was prohibitive or even inhibiting. Most of the fourteenth-century foundations begun by a peer through a licence to alienate were not bought very dearly. The licences which permitted the Montagues to found and to endow Bisham were obtained *gratis*: so were those given to the FitzAlans for Arundel college. While John Cobham paid £30 for the licence which led to the erection of Cobham College, subsequent licences were either free or bought for small sums.[45] Neither the Wakes nor the Clintons were charged for the licences enabling them to endow their foundations at Haltem-price and Maxstoke, respectively.

Grants to the friars were always licensed without charge: this may have been a tribute to their popularity, or because the alienations were of such little intrinsic value. But generally both smaller and larger fines seem to have been charged without regard for the order or the type of institution receiving the benefaction. No rule or policy is discernible. No order or branch of the church was either favoured or discriminated against in terms of fees paid for licences to alienate.

In Richard II's reign the recipients of 23 (of 52) licences paid a fee. Of these, twelve paid £10 or more, and another was charged £9. No reason for this high incidence of large fees is apparent, nor can it be deduced from an examination of the contents of the licences. As much as £40 was paid for such ordinary alienations as that of an acre of land, a rood and 3 perches, and the advowson of the parish church of Goring, made by Richard FitzAlan in 1381.[46] Possibly the king's government felt that if these large fees could be charged the number of licences applied for would decrease—or perhaps it sought, by means of higher fees, to diminish the number of alienations. It is impossible to say that the increased fees for licences caused their number to diminish; they had been falling off since 1348, and even now only 45 per cent of them had to be paid for. But the higher fees may have helped guarantee that the fall in numbers would not be reversed.

Most of those in Richard II's reign who paid handsomely were from the ranks of the great nobility—Percy, FitzAlan, Mortimer, Beauchamp, Vere, Mowbray, Montague. De Vere paid 20 marks

[44] *CPR 1361–64*, p. 139.
[45] *CPR 1361–64*, p. 265.
[46] *CPR 1381–85*, p. 38.

for a licence in 1383, and 10 marks in 1392. The king's partiality to him did not save him from considerable expense. But he, like the others listed here, could well afford to pay if he chose to. Some of the lesser nobles, however, may have felt that the new scale of fees was beyond their casual philanthropies. Families such as Willoughby, Grey, Cobham, Hastings, and Greystoke had all made endowments late in Edward III's reign. If such as they were now scared off by the high fees it would help explain the diminished number of licences. There is no correlation between family wealth and the granting of licences without fees. At all times through both centuries most licences were issued without charge.[47] Thus it is hard to attribute too much policy to any trend we have been able to spot.

The high ratio of licences with fees continued through the fifteenth century: 10 of 23 licences issued by Henry IV and Henry V, 25 of 49 for the reign of Henry VI (a generous supporter of ecclesiastical benefaction, if there ever was one), and 12 of 21 issued after 1460. Again, many of these payments were in excess of £10. As in Richard II's day, the great families and the great individual example of patronage, e.g. the Cromwell college at Tattershall, tend to be the high payers. On the other hand, apart from the £300 paid by the Beauchamps in 1481,[48] the two largest fees paid to obtain licences came from the Botreaux family. They paid 200 marks to convert a parish church into a college in 1423, and 120 marks to establish the Botreaux-Hungerford chantry in Salisbury Cathedral in 1472.[49] But taken licence by licence, the actual fees charged through the course of the fifteenth century present no pattern. All of them were paid to the hanaper.[50] If we could discern some policy behind the fees, some governmental attitude towards the question of alienations might be discovered. This is assuming there was a policy and there is but little evidence to support such a view.

When a specific piece of property or advowson was being alienated, the licence often did not state its value. This, given the licence's purpose, is not necessarily strange. The inquisition *ad quod damnum*

[47] William de Bohun received a licence for which he was to pay, but he subsequently received a 'pardon . . . of 40 marks which he promised to pay the king for this letter of licence': *CPR 1350–54*, p. 188. This was unusual, though Ralph Stafford's fine was reduced, 'at the supplication of the earl', from £10 to 10 marks: *CPR 1367–70*, p. 395.

[48] *CPR 1477–85*, p. 276.

[49] *CPR 1422–29*, pp. 189–90; *CPR 1467–77*, p. 311.

[50] The one exception was when the Earl of Warwick paid £20 to the chamber: *CPR 1348–50*, p. 565.

itself was directed at ascertaining by what tenure the land was held, rather than its worth. General licences to alienate were different, for in them the maximum amount to be alienated was designated, eventually to be realized through future grants, each needing its own licence (and being counted separately in Table 8). The values of the property were given when the subsequent alienations were made toward satisfaction of the total sum named in the general licence, for then the king had an interest in seeing that the sum of the parts did not exceed the permitted whole. Then the values were duly noted: a messuage in Canterbury of the yearly value of 3s 4d, to St Martin's, Dover, in part satisfaction of the £10 land and rent which Ralph Basset of Drayton had licence to alienate to that house.[51]

In some cases the property was being alienated as one grant permitted under a general licence. Then the specific licence might state the value of this alienation and go on to state that it is in satisfaction of a sum greater than its actual value. This procedure was not uncommon: there are about twelve instances of it in the fourteenth century, ten in the fifteenth. An acre of land and the advowson of Attenborough Church, of the yearly value of 60s 2d, are alienated by a licence which declares them to be in full satisfaction of an earlier licence to alienate 100s worth of land and rents.[52] A piece of land worth £7 11s 2d and a rental of £1 8s 10d are together named as being in satisfaction of £10 towards the £20 of land and rent Haltemprice Canonry was licensed to acquire from Thomas Wake of Lidell.[53] Even medieval accounting practices did not mistake the sum of £9 for £10. Sometimes this 'adjustment' between stated value and the value of satisfaction was as much as 50 per cent. In a few instances the value of the alienated property was explicitly stated to be less than the assessed amount: land and rent of a clear value of £7 are in satisfaction of a licence, to the extent of 20 marks.[54] Was the king trying to restrict the passage of land into mortmain, as per the statute of 1279? If so he was neither doing it effectively nor efficiently. There is no indication that the nobles failed to obtain licences when they sought them, or failed to get permission to alienate as much as they cared to. And no one imposes a policy by implementing it in some two dozen cases out of over 400.

[51] *CPR 1327–30*, p. 359.
[52] *CPR 1338–40*, p. 203.
[53] *CPR 1340–43*, p. 529.
[54] *CPR 1429–36*, p. 100.

L

Licences were issued when one exchanged property with the church, since what was now granted away was passing into mortmain, though not strictly as a form of philanthropy. These transactions were more in the way of property transfers, since there is no evidence that the church invariably profited by receiving more than it surrendered. Some exchanges must have been equitable enough, as was William Montague's straight trade of 2-acre plots in an Oxfordshire village, in 1341, with the nuns of Godstow.[55] A few licences explicitly state the exchange to be of 'the like quantity out of land'.[56] Many were so close as to make little difference: 10 acres of land in exchange for 7, plus a bit of moor and an alder grove.[57] One licence stipulated that the 4 acres received by John Mowbray were worth more than the messuage and $2\frac{1}{2}$ acres of arable which he had granted to the parish priest of Epworth.[58] Richard FitzAlan traded a Warwickshire advowson for the inn, 'Pulteneysyn', in London. But exchange played only a small role in the story of land passing into mortmain, and whether these few transactions were balanced ones or not seems of little matter. There is no indication that any of the exchanges were made under coercion, or that the licence to alienate served to cover a purchase of land by an ecclesiastical institution.[59]

Before the licence was issued the escheator in the county in which the property lay held an inquisition. Here the conditions of tenure were determined. We can assume that most property alienated by the nobility was held in chief. Some licences were issued in expressed anticipation of favourable results from the inquisition, and we know of no cancellations because of the findings of a hearing. Some few licences do attest that the property in question was held in chief, but others carry *carte blanche* approval, in anticipation: 'whether held in chief or not'.[60]

The escheator's job was to determine those conditions. The statute of 1279 had forbidden the alienation of *all* land in the realm, even if held 'not . . . immediately of the king'.[61] Most property in towns was held in burgage, variously referred to as free burgage and burgage in

---

[55] *CPR 1313–17*, p. 89.
[56] *CPR 1330–34*, p. 52.
[57] *CPR 1334–38*, p. 535. Similar exchanges can be found: *CPR 1334–38*, p. 552; *CPR 1350–54*, p. 122.
[58] *CPR 1330–34*, p. 543.
[59] For a contrary opinion, Wood-Legh: *op. cit.*, pp. 72–3.
[60] *CPR 1330–34*, pp. 177, 179; *CPR 1345–48*, p. 444; *CPR 1361–64*, p. 402.
[61] *CPR 1436–41*, p. 78.

chief. One messuage in Cambridge was held in free burgage by a service of 2*d*, 'gavel'.[62] Possessions held in burgage tenure were alienated in towns both great and small: land and rent in Bristol, a plot in 'the' suburb of London, a London inn, 4 messuages and 2 tofts in Arundel, a messuage in Carlisle, and an advowson in Connings-yard.[63] Other bits of land were held by other forms of tenure: a toft, arable, meadow and pasture near Hull in socage; land in London held in fee simple; land in Kent held in fealty and of the service of 2*s* 6*d* per annum, etc.[64] Henry Vavasour alienated an advowson which he held from Queen Philippa as of the castle and honour of Ponte-fract.[65] Henry Percy granted some bits of land 'said to be parcel of his manor of Semer, held of the king in chief by the service of one-thirtieth part of a knight's fee'.[66]

If the king did not refuse to issue licences when the nobles sought (and were willing to pay for) them, his officials at least were concerned lest he suffer loss without prior knowledge. An alienation into mortmain, after all, meant that the land would henceforth never escheat,[67] and that the feudal dues and services would be lost forever. The king was reminded of this. But James Faucomberge was licensed to make an alienation notwithstanding.[68] Licences were granted 'although after inquisition *ad quod damnum* the sheriff . . . returns that it is to the king's prejudice'.[69] Sometimes the fees had to be paid in order that the petitioner might make a prejudicial alienation; but once again, any policy behind the fees escapes detection. There is no reason to think that the king, through the use of fees, tried to recoup any real financial losses which he may have suffered because of even the most prejudicial alienations. The concept of real property, dis-posable at will during its 'owner's' lifetime, seems to lie just below the surface. If the forms surrounding alienation were complied with,[70]

---

[62] *CPR 1384–50*, p. 105.

[63] *CPR 1348–50*, p. 49; *ibid.*, p. 512; *CPR 1377–81*, p. 351; *CPR 1381–85*, pp. 527–8; *CPR 1391–96*, p. 562; *CPR 1408–13*, pp. 426–7.

[64] *CPR 1401–5*, p. 111; *ibid.*, p. 175; *CPR 1374–77*, p. 117.

[65] *CPR 1330–34*, p. 103.

[66] *CPR 1327–30*, p. 383.

[67] Though after Peter Mauley had alienated land to the convent of Grosmont in Eskdale the alienation was allowed 'on condition that on each new creation of a prior of the house, the prior do fealty to the king by reason of the service so remitted': *CPR 1350–54*, p. 70.

[68] *CPR 1338–40*, p. 55.

[69] *CPR 1307–13*, p. 233.

[70] Though these forms might extend to petitioning in Parliament for the necessary licence: *CPR 1436–41*, pp. 55–6, 167.

and any rather arbitrarily levied fee or fine paid, the nobles were in fact free to do much as they pleased with their possessions, in so far as the licences to alienate offer any insight. Land went steadily into mortmain, and the kings never took serious steps to stop it.[71] Whatever the reason for the decreasing number of alienations in the fifteenth century, royal policy was not responsible.

Table 8 illustrated the ever diminishing share of the number of alienations which went to the regular orders. Table 10 offers some analysis in terms of the types of recipients of the licences, with a further breakdown of category of regular orders. It shows us that the

TABLE 10   Percentage of types of recipients of licences, by century

| Century | Benedic-tines | Other regulars | Types of order | | | |
			Canons	Friars	Nuns	Hospitals
Fourteenth	9	25	16	13	12	0*
	(210)†	(80)	(289)	(184)	(140)	(475)
Fifteenth	1	7	5	1	0	0*
	(152)	(84)	(277)	(184)	(137)	(564)

* The number of hospitals receiving licences in the fourteenth century was six, in the fifteenth, three. Each comes to less than 0·5 per cent and so rounds out at 0.

† The numbers in parentheses represent the number of houses within that type of order. Figures are from Knowles and Hadcock: *Medieval Religious Houses*. Fourteenth-century totals are for the period 1350–1422, fifteenth-century ones for the period 1422–1500.

diminished number of alienations in the fifteenth century was tantamount to a virtual neglect of most regular houses and orders. In the fourteenth century 9 per cent of the Benedictine houses in England had received alienations from the nobles, whereas in the fifteenth century only 1 per cent of the houses so benefited. In number, nineteen Benedictine houses received twenty-six licences in the fourteenth century, while only two houses even got one grant apiece in the fifteenth century. The other monastic orders and the orders of canons regular had a comparable drop in the percentage of the members receiving licences, from 25 per cent to 7 per cent and from 16 per cent to 5 per cent, respectively. The mendicants went from 13 per cent to 1 per cent, i.e. from twenty-four recipient houses to two, and the nuns (with whom are included the canonesses) went from 12 per

[71] Though the authorities could be energetic enough when they chose. Chew: *op. cit.*, p. 11.

cent to 0 per cent, i.e. from seventeen recipients to none at all.[72]

To the social historian of religion these are very sobering statistics. They indicate that by the end of the middle ages the higher ranks of society turned very sharply away from the general level of support they had once, in the not far distant past, given to the regular orders. We cannot say how serious the defection really was for the church, in terms of the over-all financial situation, for we have no way of knowing if increasing support from lesser strata of lay society acted as a balancing mechanism. But this would seem to be an unlikely possibility. There were real problems within the church: it was over-extended, in terms of popular support for its physical plant, if not in other ways touching upon its spiritual values.

To know the percentages of houses within an order which received alienations tells us nothing about how popular specific members of that order might be. In aggregate about 240 separate institutions—regular houses, churches, chapels, hospitals, nunneries, etc.—profited from the 396 licences to alienate that were directed to identifiable beneficiaries. Some of the recipients were the pet project of a noble family, e.g. the Austin canonry at Bisham, the Franciscan nunnery at Denney, the canonry at Haltemprice, etc. If they were a *de novo* foundation, the full tale of their endowment is told above. They received many licences. Thus we see that the overwhelming majority of houses and churches which figure in Table 3 benefited from but a single alienation. Several Austin canonries were founded or championed by the nobles: forty-six canonries shared ninety-three licences in the fourteenth century. But even in this preferred category we see the decline in time, for in the fifteenth century only fourteen houses were favoured, with but sixteen licences. To catch even the passing fancy of one noble benefactor had come to be more a stroke of fortune than a matter of course for most recipients. We have seen that many alienations represented but a slight increase in wealth at that. Of course, an alienation bringing a rent of £4 per annum, hardly of much value to a monastery, would be a substantial boon to a parish church. Small secular institutions, if endowed by a peer even to this minimal extent, stood to profit relatively more than a great and ancient foundation. Such famous Benedictine houses as Reading, St Albans, and Bury St Edmunds received one noble alienation apiece through the entire period. They had been relegated, along with scores of other old houses, to the back-waters of the public religi-

[72] Eileen Power: *Medieval English Nunneries* (Cambridge, 1922), p. 472.

ous consciousness, and they were usually ignored by the aristocracy.

At the other end of the spectrum, no type of religious order ever saw more than 25 per cent of its members receive alienations from the nobles, and most groups came nothing near this figure. If we exclude the hospitals from the calculation, we see that in the fourteenth century 126 licences were granted to 903 houses: 14 per cent were recipients. In the fifteenth century the numbers are 27 licences, 834 potential recipients—3 per cent. But at best we must accept that the nobles were not the main prop on which the financial basis of the church was built. Two other sources of support bore much of the burden. One was the rest of lay society. The other, and most important, was the accumulated and preserved wealth of the church, the land which had been going into mortmain since Anglo-Saxon times. No single century and no single group in society contributed the bulk of the wealth. The role of time and the church's institutional immortality were of paramount importance.

Except in the royal duchies of Cornwall and Cheshire and in sparsely populated Westmorland, institutions in every county benefited from alienations. The north held its own, and no other county could approach Yorkshire in terms of the number of houses which profited from alienations. Wales received but five grants. No English peer made a grant of English land to any Scottish foundation, and only a few went to Irish houses. Local loyalties, tied to local power and status, were the overriding motive force in determining both the recipient and the site of the alienation. Men thought of themselves as being tied to places—the land, the local institutions, the people—when they turned to charitable activities.[73]

The south-west witnessed no great wave of aristocratic benefaction. Devon, Dorset, and Somerset each had a few favoured establishments. The Courtenays were minor donors in Devon, and the family of FitzPayn made small grants in Dorset and Somerset. Somerset profited most from noble benefactions: of nine institutions there receiving lands and advowsons, eight got their gifts in the fourteenth century. The only fifteenth-century grant was for the conversion of North Cadbury parish church into a secular college, in 1423, by William and Elizabeth Botreaux. This part of England saw the erection of no great noble foundations, and no house enjoyed the prolonged attention of any single noble family.

[73] R. S. Schofield: 'The Geographical Distribution of Wealth in England, 1334–1649', *Economic History Review*, 2nd series, XVIII (1965), pp. 483–510.

West country peers took care of their own. Gloucester, including Bristol, received many endowments. The Berkeleys were particularly lavish there: of the twelve alienations they made in the fourteenth century, ten were for Gloucestershire establishments.[74] The Despensers and Bohuns were benefactors of more than one house. Only four alienations went to Worcester churches—three by the Beauchamps, and all before 1350. The Mortimers were active in Hereford and Shropshire. The Abbey at Haughmond was unusually favoured, receiving alienations from the Charltons, FitzAlans, Cliffords, and Lord LeStraunge. Very few institutions drew diversified support like this. Most houses had but one family to look after its fortunes. Neither in Hampshire nor in Wiltshire were many alienations made: four institutions per county, with only Salisbury Cathedral getting more than one grant. Of the nine alienations made in the two counties, five came after 1422.

The ecclesiastical foundations of Kent were much in the public eye. Eight establishments there received alienations, with regular houses coming in for a considerable share of the riches. The Benedictines at Faversham, Canterbury, Dover, and Rochester all got one licensed alienation apiece. All these endowments were fourteenth century ones. Two Austin houses, at Badlesmere and at Tunbridge, were also remembered. The Cobham family was busy, founding a college at Cobham and endowing a chantry chapel at Rochester.

The Shoreham Carmelites were given land, in 1348, by John Mowbray. Otherwise, Sussex was only remembered by its great resident family, the FitzAlans. They supported the Austins at Tortington (four licences to them between 1334 and 1395), the gild of St Mary at Horsham, the Dominicans and the alien Benedictine priory at Arundel. This was in addition to their creation of Holy Trinity College, Arundel, and a hospital there, for which no fewer than seven separate licences were issued between 1375 and 1395. This was local proprietary interest with a vengeance.

Neither the counties around London nor the city itself were focal points for benefaction from the nobles through alienations. They were apt to be most generous where their lands, homes, and family traditions were, and where, locally, they were exalted far beyond their national importance. Around London both the king and the great bourgeois fortunes offered competition to their wealth and social

---

[74] Dugdale: *Baronage*, I, 358–9, and J. Smyth (ed. J. Maclean): *The Berkeley Manuscripts—The Lives of the Berkeleys* (Bristol, 1883–5), 3 volumes.

pretensions. Furthermore, they owned little land in the city, beyond their own town houses. The modern dormitory areas of London were not much more popular: two recipients in Bedfordshire (though Warden Abbey got three alienations from the St Amands), three in Hertfordshire, and three in Surrey. Three Middlesex monasteries received alienations: the royal house of St Saviour, Syon, the nunnery at Stratford, and Westminster Abbey (two grants). More alienations went into Berkshire, but two houses there were special projects—the church at Hungerford and the Montague canonry at Bisham. St George's chapel, Windsor, was popular; Beauchamp and Bohun both endowed it at the time of its foundation, and others followed suit. Buckinghamshire, more socially remote from London and not under the influence of any great noble family, did contain three regular houses, three chapels, a secular college, and a friary that were enriched. London itself did not attract many alienations, though many nobles left personal property to convents and churches there, and many chose to be buried in the great metropolis. London provides the extreme disparity between patterns of endowment through alienations and other forms of benefactions—between what one did when one was in the midst of life and when one was dying. We have seen that deathbed thoughts often turned to London.

As reflected in the licences to alienate, noble generosity ran high in East Anglia. Grants to new foundations, e.g. Clare College, as well as to older houses, e.g. those at Ely, Earls Colne, Saffron Walden, etc., are all found. The families of Burgh, Vere, Valence, Bohun, and Bourchier all gave more than once. In Norfolk and Suffolk together twenty-nine different institutions received grants, with nine of them benefiting more than once. These two counties were such focal points of benefaction that not only are the great local families found among the patrons, e.g. Ufford, Bourchier, Mowbray, de la Pole, Warrenne, etc., but alienations came from such foreigners as Montague, Beauchamp, Audley, Scales, and Botetourt. The area was unusually rich in the number of regular houses that attracted noble attention. Only nine of the twenty-nine recipient institutions were secular ones. Most of the licences were issued in the fourteenth century: 20 of the 26 for Norfolk houses, 10 of the 17 for Suffolk ones (or 30 of 43 in all).

The Midlands are a diversified and arbitrary area, and generalizations are not so readily made. Derbyshire was not an important centre of religious life, and only two convents and one chapel received alienations. This lack of prominence is also true for Northampton and Nottingham. In Stafford two convents, two parish churches, a hospital, and a friary all received grants, all before 1353. Of seven alienations made there, two were from the Staffords. The Zouches and the Ferrers were both generous in fourteenth-century Leicestershire, though six of the eight recipients got but one grant. There was more activity in Oxfordshire: the Ewelme alms-house, the gild at Thame, the Percy alienations to University College, Oxford, the monastery of St Frideswide, and the Franciscan house in Oxford. Except for the Percy grant, there were no mortmain alienations, in either century, to Oxford University or any of its colleges or halls. The Beauchamps were munificent in Warwickshire. They alienated land to the collegiate church of St Mary, Warwick, which they rebuilt to splendid proportions (and in which many of them were buried), to the Warwick Dominicans, to the hospital of St John there, to the regulars at Kenilworth, to the chapel of Guyscliff, to Astley College, and to Maxstoke Priory. The Astleys, Clintons, and Zouches gave to these and other establishments within the county, though almost exclusively in the fourteenth century.

The nobles gave to Lincolnshire houses with great generosity. Twenty-two Lincoln institutions profited from 41 licences: two-thirds of these (27 of 41) in the fourteenth century. But in contrast with East Anglia, exactly half the 22 recipients were secular establishments (including Lincoln Cathedral, with seven licences). The secular houses did significantly better in the fifteenth century than did the regular: of the fourteen alienations made in the latter century, ten went to secular houses. These figures include the fifteenth-century endowments to the Cromwell collegiate foundation at Tattershall, and the Mowbray foundation (of a Carthusian house) at Epworth in the 1390s. Besides these families, Kyme, Beaumont, Willoughby, and Roos were especially prominent. Beaumont and Roos each helped four different institutions, Willoughby and Kyme three each.

The North was provided for by its own barons. Ogle, Greystoke and Moulton made alienations in Cumberland. The Nevilles were active in Durham, alienating land to the Cathedral in the late fourteenth century, founding and endowing Staindrop College in 1408. The Percys were the only noble donors in their quasi-kingdom of Northumberland. But it is in Yorkshire that the gentle current of noble alienations becomes a torrent. There 59 alienations were divided among 34 houses. Of these, 47 were made in the fourteenth century, 35 to regular houses and friaries, 12 to secular institutions. The twelve alienations made in the fifteenth century were evenly split between seculars and regulars. These totals represent endowment on an unparalleled scale. Yorkshire was very much a land carved into spheres of influence between the great lineages, and they had their favourite beneficiaries. Roos, Scrope, Everingham, Lisle, Mauley, FitzHugh, Wake, etc., share the honours, if on a lesser scale, with Percy and Neville. Only two houses, the Franciscans at Richmond and the Carthusians at Hull, had more than one noble family among its benefactors. Scrope and Neville both gave small bits of land to the Friars Minor, while Scrope and others twice joined the de la Poles in endowing the new Charterhouse at Hull. Yorkshire was hardly a land of joint enterprises.[75] The Wakes, for example, received twelve licences to alienate property to Haltemprice Abbey between 1331 and 1373. No other family made any other endowment of mortmain property to that house. This in a microcosm is the story of how the noble families did not interact in their philanthropic activity.

This geographical glance at the alienations reveals how voluntary activities were really the result of a process of decision making from among a number of seemingly imperative alternatives. To give in London or nearer home? to an old house—to which one might or might not be tied by family tradition—or to a new one? etc. In most cases nobles made their alienations from property within the same or an adjoining county, though alienations to St Paul's might come from Norfolk and Huntingdon as well as from closer at hand. The location of territory had to be balanced against the ability of the new ecclesiastical 'owner' to collect the revenues. Larger institutions, with a more sophisticated bureaucratic complex, might welcome land in a distant part of the realm, while such a donation would have been of no practical value had it been made to a local chapel or parish church. We must not forget that formulae about acreage meant actual land in the fields, worked or farmed by peasants. The gifts of the nobles were governed in part by considerations of place, as their inclinations were at least partially formed by their own spatial orientation to their lands, their houses and castles, the religious houses wherein they prayed, their chosen churches of burial, and the seat of the king's government.

[75] Charles Ross: 'The Yorkshire Baronage, 1399–1485', Oxford D. Phil. thesis, 1951, p. xvii: 'in spite of their widespread estates, the baronage retained strong local roots.'

Lastly, we consider the alienations in terms of the families involved. Almost every noble family received at least one licence. Of those few that did not, several were quite minor and their absence from the list does not strike us as being of particular importance or interest. This holds true of Bonville, Camoys, Mautravers, Tuchet, Welles, and Wenlock.[76] But the Bohuns and the Tiptofts were of some prominence, and if St John was never a major family within the peerage, it was a long-lived one. Of course, alienations in mortmain were but one form of benefaction, and no licences to alienate hardly means no philanthropy. But if they were not necessarily the most important form of benefaction, they were the most commonly used. Unlike testamentary dispositions, property alienated during the donor's life might have affected his status in a way that gifts from his property, after death, would not. There were numerous compensations for the financial sacrifices incumbent upon one making an alienation. So the failure of some families ever to seek and to receive letters patent is at least worth passing notice.

On the other hand we must not wax too poetic over a nobility precipitously alienating its treasured and hard-built accumulations of real property. Of the 89 noble families obtaining royal licences, 51 made 3 or fewer alienations. Fifteen families made 4 to 6 alienations, 8 families made 7 to 9 alienations, 6 made between 10 and 14, and only 9 noble families made over 15 alienations. Families made many or most, though rarely all their benefactions, to one or two pet institutions, often to new or thoroughly rebuilt ones. This is true for almost all the really large donors. Alienations tended to be made, within a family, in clusters within a short period, with perhaps an interval of some years before someone else in the family became active again. These two patterns are interrelated, and they serve to emphasize that even in the most charitably inclined and churchy families benefaction depended largely upon the impulse of one or two individuals, more than upon a continuing and self-sustaining family tradition. But these are only tendencies, not iron-clad rules.

Thomas Astley furnished a good, if rather extreme example of these connected phenomena. In all he received six licences to alienate. The first was in 1337, the last in 1343. All were for the enrichment and enlargement of the chantry chapel of the Virgin Mary in the church of Astley, Warwickshire. Astley lived until 1366, but his role

[76] Though Lord Wenlock received no licences to alienate, he did rebuild the church at Luton: *VCH Bedford*, II, 368.

as an ecclesiastical benefactor, as reflected through licences to alienate, ended when the college was completed. The Lords Zouche of Harringworth were peers of the realm through virtually the entire fourteenth century, but of the eleven licences they received, six came in the 1340s. However, in this case the beneficiaries were a diverse lot: two alienations to the Pipewell Cistercians, two to a chantry in Warwickshire, one to Studley Priory, and one to be divided among two different chantries. Other family grants, before and after that active decade, went to different houses and churches, with no place receiving more than one alienation. The Lords Lisle made all seven of the licensed alienations between 1331 and 1354: four to the Abbey at Bolton in Craven, York, and one each to Norwich Cathedral, St Oswald's in Nostell, York, and to their own foundation, a chantry chapel at Harewood, York.

For the most part only the great families were really in the forefront in terms of the number of licences obtained. To make more than fifteen alienations both a pet project (or a number of them—witness the FitzAlans and the de la Poles) and a strong family tradition were usually needed. Beauchamp, FitzAlan, Montague, Percy, and de la Pole are the names we find on this list. The new foundations of these and other families have been discussed, but such great enterprises were usually needed to put a family in the category of really big donors. Other major benefactors include the Clintons and the Wakes. A lesser family, the Berkeleys, was a donor of major scope in the fourteenth century (with twelve licences between 1315 and 1385), but absolutely none afterwards, though they continued to be summoned to Parliament through the fifteenth century. And they achieved this high level of munificence without a *de novo* foundation to their credit. The Bassets received ten licences to alienate between 1319 and 1385. Only their demise limited their activity.

The great families gave both generously and over a long period of time. The first Beauchamp licence was received in 1308, and the last in 1418. The first Montague licence came in 1312, the last in 1414, the first Percy one in 1313, the last in 1462. Some of these houses made most of their grants in the fourteenth century. Only four of the 19 Beauchamp alienations were after 1399: 2 of the 21 made by the FitzAlans. Only one of the 21 Montague alienations came after 1399, though they at least died out, in the male line, in 1428. Exceptions to this fourteenth-century bias are furnished by the two northern giants, Neville and Percy. Of the 22 Neville alienations, 14 were licensed after

1399: 9 of 19 Percy grants were from the fifteenth century. And the de la Poles, only entering the scene in Richard II's reign, came on with a rush and made 16 of their 21 grants after 1399.

As some families display a prominence here out of all proportion to their national role, e.g. Wake, Zouche, and Roos (with seven alienations to their credit between 1307 and 1361), so others are striking by their lack of activity. The Beauforts received but one licence. The Beaumonts received two in all, the first in 1317 and the second in 1414. The Courtenays received five licences in all, and every one came between 1309 and 1350. The five to the de Veres were scattered through the fourteenth century. Both these families were now more concerned with consolidation than expansion. The de Veres had once had a great tradition of benefaction and patronage, and Essex is still rich with monastic remains and monastic towns first erected with de Vere money and blessings. Though in their wills they continued to honour traditional family obligations, they were chary of new commitments. The Despensers received but three licences, for all their political activity. Piers Gaveston made no alienations, though Edward II made some, after Piers's death, specifically for the sake of his soul. The Staffords avoided even a suspicion of enthusiasm and only sued for seven licences, five in the fourteenth century, and only two in the fifteenth, when their fortunes rose so high. The Woodvilles only made one alienation, in 1480.

Was political prominence, being related as it was to wealth and proprietary connections, completely unrelated to a propensity to endow? No direct and simple correlation exists. Nor, it would seem, were intellectual interests any reliable guide to the rate of endowment. In fact, none of the traditional polarizations—court or country, north or south, old family or new family, or even great noble family as against small family—seems to offer a sure key to plotting the path of benefaction. Individuals, with their idiosyncrasies, seem to have been a key determinant. With about ninety families making some 450 alienations, it is obvious that, apart from a few favourite foundations, few ecclesiastical institutions were greatly enriched. Most of the approximately forty families making more than three alienations spread them among more than one recipient. The case of the Botetourts is by no means unique: four grants in twenty years went to four different recipients. No one got very rich from this type of activity. Even great families sprinkled a single alienation among their more systematic enrichments. In general, there seem to have been alienations that were part of a prolonged effort to build a single institution, and those that were made without system or scheme. These latter, the most numerous (particularly in the fourteenth century) and the most common in terms of the number of families engaged in making them, rarely represented a great gain for the recipient, or a great sacrifice for the donor. Licences to alienate are an index of the willingness of the nobles to make endowments to the church. Beyond that the ground is uncertain.

Appendix II

Tables with raw numbers

THE data expressed in some of the tables in the text in percentages are given here in raw numbers. Table A1 below has data which are shown in Tables 3, 4, and 5 in the text; Table A2 is the basis for Table 8, A3 for Table 10, and A4 also for Table 10.

A1 Grants to chantries

| Years | Recipients | | | | | | Total grants | Value | | Size | | Duration | |
	Secular	Cathedral	Regular	Mendicants	Misc.	Unknown		Under £5	£5 or more	1 man	larger	1 year	Over 1 year
1307–27	9	1	6	0	0	1	17*	2	4	8	5	1	1
1327–48	41	4	22	2	2	5	76	13	30	27	30	0	1
1348–77	23	6	17	1	5	2	54	3	18	12	9	0	4
1377–99	10	5	9	1	1	2	28	1	12	9	15	4	5
1399–1422	14	3	5	0	2	3	27	1	15	7	14	4	8
1422–60	28	6	7	2	3	4	50	3	28	15	25	1	19
1460–85	15	2	2	5	2	3	29	5	17	15	8	4	11
Total	140	27	68	11	15	20	281	28	124	93	116	14	48

* The sources do not give all the itemized information for any category. Consequently, no sub-totals equal the total number of grants.

A2 Licences permitting alienations in mortmain, by years and recipients

	Recipients					
Years	Regulars	Nuns	Friars	Seculars	Misc.	Total licences
1307–27	26	2	8	10	2	48
1327–48	81	3	16	56	13	169
1348–77	36	7	8	28	5	84
1377–99	24	0	6	18	4	52
1399–1422	12	0	0	10	1	23
1422–60	13	0	1	33	2	49
1460–85	4	0	1	15	1	21
Total	196	12	40	170	28	446

A3 Types of recipients of licences, by century

	Number of recipient houses within various types of orders						
Century	Benedictines	Other regulars	Canons	Friars	Nuns	Hospitals	Secular institutions
Fourteenth	19 (210)*	20 (80)	46 (289)	24 (184)	17 (140)	6 (475)	78
Fifteenth	2 (152)	6 (84)	14 (277)	2 (184)	0 (137)	3 (564)	42

* The numbers in parentheses represent the number of houses within that type of order.

A4 Number of licences to alienate granted to types of orders, by century

	Number of licences to types of recipients						
Century	Benedictines	Other regulars	Canons	Friars	Nuns	Hospitals	Secular institutions
Fourteenth	26	30	93	30	29	6	117
Fifteenth	2	11	16	2	0	3	57

Index

STUDIES IN SOCIAL HISTORY

edited by

HAROLD PERKIN

Professor of Social History, University of Lancaster

◇◇◇